ANDRÉ GREEN
at The *Squiggle* Foundation

Winnicott Studies Monograph Series

The Person Who Is Me:
Contemporary Perspectives on the True and False Self
edited by Val Richards

Fathers, Families, and the Outside World
edited by Val Richards

The *Squiggle* Foundation is a registered charity
set up in 1981 to study and cultivate the tradition
of D. W. Winnicott. For further information, contact
The Administrator, 33 Amberley Road, London N13 4BH.
Tel: 020 8882 9744; Fax: 020 8886 2418

Winnicott Studies Monograph Series

ANDRÉ GREEN
at The *Squiggle* Foundation

edited by

Jan Abram

London & New York
KARNAC BOOKS
for
The *Squiggle* Foundation

First published in 2000 by
H. Karnac (Books) Ltd., 58 Gloucester Road, London SW7 4QY
A subsidiary of Other Press LLC, New York

Copyright © 2000 The *Squiggle* Foundation
Editor's foreword copyright © 2000 Jan Abram
Lectures copyright © 2000 André Green

The rights of André Green and Jan Abram to be identified as the authors of this work have been asserted in accordance with §§ 77 and 78 of the Copyright Design and Patents Act 1988.

All rights reserved. No part of this publication may be reproduced, stored in a retrieval system, or transmitted, in any form or by any means, electronic, mechanical, photocopying, recording, or otherwise, without the prior written permission of the publisher.

British Library Cataloguing in Publication Data

A C.I.P. for this book is available from the British Library

ISBN 1 85575 182 8

10 9 8 7 6 5 4 3 2 1

Edited, designed, and produced by Communication Crafts

Printed in Great Britain by Polestar AUP Aberdeen Limited

www.karnacbooks.com

In memory of Marion Milner

CONTENTS

ACKNOWLEDGEMENTS viii

ABOUT THE AUTHOR AND EDITOR ix

EDITOR'S FOREWORD by *Jan Abram* xi

1 Experience and thinking in analytic practice   1

2 Object(s) and subject   17

3 On thirdness   39

4 The posthumous Winnicott: on *Human Nature*   69

5 The intuition of the negative in *Playing and Reality*   85

REFERENCES   107

INDEX   111

ACKNOWLEDGEMENTS

Cesare Sacerdoti of Karnac Books, and a Patron of The *Squiggle* Foundation, suggested the idea for this collection some time ago. *Squiggle* is fortunate and grateful indeed for his sound judgement, enthusiasm, and encouragement.

Squiggle is indebted to André Green's agreement to publish the papers as well as the huge amount of work he took in refining and adding to the texts. Also a Patron of *Squiggle*, Dr Green's long-standing association with the Foundation has enriched our thinking and discussion on Winnicott's work.

A big thank you to Graham Sleight, General Manager of Karnac Books, and many thanks to Carole Lee-Robbins, who achieved the difficult task of typing up the papers from the audiotapes.

Finally, special thanks to Klara King of Communication Crafts for her meticulous copyediting.

ABOUT THE AUTHOR AND EDITOR

ANDRÉ GREEN is a Training Analyst for the Paris Psychoanalytic Society where he has also been the former President and Director of the Paris Psychoanalytic Institute. Dr Green was also Vice President of the International Psychoanalytical Society and Professor of University College London, for the Freud Memorial Chair. Presently he is an honorary Professor at the Buenos Aires University, Member of the Moscow Academy of Humanities Research, and Member of the New York Academy of Sciences.

He has written numerous articles and books, including *The Tragic Effect, On Private Madness, La folie privée*. His recent publications in English are referred to at the end of the Foreword and in the list of references at the end of the book.

JAN ABRAM is a psychoanalytic psychotherapist in private practice in London and an Associate member of the London Centre for Psychotherapy. Since 1989 she has worked on many courses and workshops with the *Squiggle* Foundation and was appointed Director for the period between 1996 and 2000.

The author of many papers on the work of Winnicott, Jan Abram has also published *Individual Psychotherapy Trainings: A*

Guide (1992: currently being updated for publication in 2000) and *The Language of Winnicott: A Dictionary of Winnicott's Use of Words* (1996). She teaches and lectures widely and is currently following the analytic training at The Institute of Psycho-Analysis, London.

EDITOR'S FOREWORD

"A kind of French Winnicott"

Jan Abram

*The first lecture:
absence and a piece of chocolate*

On 3 March 1987, André Green gave his first lecture to The *Squiggle* Foundation, entitled, "Experience and Thinking in Analytic Practice". Alexander Newman, the founder and first Director of *Squiggle*, introduced Dr Green and informed the audience that his collection of papers had just been published entitled *On Private Madness* (1986) and was available for sale in the bookshop. Newman followed this by saying that it was a book that he had read "from cover to cover, with little understanding and much interest". This evoked smiles and laughter from those in the audience used to Newman's dry sense of humour, and some quizzical looks from those of us who were newcomers.

André Green, quick on the uptake, said that he thought that probably Alexander Newman was really saying that he had read his book with great understanding and little interest. This was followed by a more general laughter, which probably included a sense of relief that the speaker had taken Newman's comment in the spirit in which it had been said. André Green did not stop there; he then turned to the audience, saying, "I don't know what your reactions will be in terms of understanding and interest, after this lecture, because probably I have some difficulties in understanding myself with more or less interest." Now the audience could all relax and laugh together.

The warmth, spontaneity, and humour of this exchange captured all of us who were privileged to be in the audience that day. Subsequently we were treated to a lecture that was quite breathtaking for its texture and substance, equal to the delivery of a speaker who has the gift of conveying the ineffability of the analytic situation with humanity, passion, and a special sense of humour. My recollection is that the lecture was timeless, and it seemed that nobody moved for an hour and a half. Interest is too mild a word—the audience was fascinated. As for understanding—there were many themes that probably passed many of us by. And this, I think, is what Alexander Newman and André Green were alluding to in their playful exchange: the different analytic environments between the French and Anglo-Saxon worlds. André Green's exploration of psychoanalysis holds particular qualities that are unfamiliar to a British audience. I shall come back to this point.

When listening to a new speaker discussing a familiar topic—psychoanalysis—in an unfamiliar way—French psychoanalysis—what exactly do we take away with us and why? I am struck that I came away from that lecture with some particular impressions. I felt that Dr Green was both playful and serious. His warmth and humanity was conveyed through his sense of humour, and his passion through his respect for the patient's suffering. The other seemingly banal memory I was left with was that Dr Green lived and worked in an apartment in Paris, and that he liked a piece of chocolate after his lunch. In studying the text, I came to realize that my memory relates to the denouement of the clinical illustration in the paper, where Green introduces his concept of the *negative*. The piece of chocolate relates to something happening outside the session—during the *absence* of the object (i.e. Green eating a piece of chocolate before going into the session)—and yet *within* the analytic relationship. The patient feels tantalized by what her analyst was doing in the two minutes between seeing him, not seeing him, and seeing him again (p. 12).

Green points out that there are two aspects of the *negative*. In one there is destruction and foreclosure—an attack on insight and the analytic setting—and the other, the *work of the negative* (which is instigated by the analytic relationship), contains the potential to bring the unthought known into consciousness, which will result in integration (p. 14).

What happened around the chocolate, between Green and his patient, facilitated a new shift in the patient, illustrating psychic change. "It is only if the patient can experience that feeling of movement in the session that I think he will be able to continue moving and working outside the session in the world" (p. 15).

Green does not talk about repetition, nor about enactment, but, rather, about *actualization*.[1] For Green, the analytic experience with every patient will involve actualizations of the patient's internal constructions within the analytic relationship—"What goes on between these two partners, analyst and analysand, is a historical process in that it deals with the way in which history is constituted in a person: how it works, how it becomes effective" (p. 2).

Green defines the historical thus: ". . . for the psyche, the historical could be defined as a combination of: what has happened, what has not happened, what could have happened, what has happened to someone else but not to me, what could not have happened, and finally—to summarize all these alternatives about what has happened—a statement that one would not have even dreamed of as a representation of what really happened" (pp. 2–3).

So what is the past? In Green's theory there is no such thing *per se*—rather, it is the subject's personal elaborations of the above variables. And the analytic situation lends itself to the *actualizations* of such constructions and such variables.

---

[1] Professor Joseph Sandler, a long-term colleague and friend of André Green's, also uses the term "actualization" to explore his ideas on affect and role responsiveness (Sandler, 1976a, 1976b).

The second and fifth lectures

"... you cannot speak of love unless you include an object." [p. 29]

The question of why a French psychoanalyst was visiting an organization dedicated to the study and dissemination of Winnicott's work, and why a *Squiggle* audience, whilst being very interested, may have difficulty in understanding Green's work, was addressed by Nina Farhi (the second Director of *Squiggle*, between 1989 and 1996), three years after the first lecture. By now *Squiggle* audiences were hooked, and on 2 June 1990, André Green presented to us his second lecture, entitled "Object(s) and Subject". Nina Farhi, in her introduction to the talk, commented on the difference between the traditions and qualities of the French and English cultural heritages, with the English traditions celebrating empiricism and pragmatism and the French, intellectualism and abstraction. Nina went on to say how André Green recognizes the deep abstraction to be found in Winnicott's work and that *Playing and Reality* (1971b) "is one of the most fundamental works in the field of psychoanalysis which embraces both traditions". It is striking how these words anticipated Green's paper of 1997 (the fifth in this collection), in which he explores and illustrates Winnicott's intuitive understanding of the themes pertaining to the *negative*. In fact Green begins this paper by saying that one of the sources that guided him to the introduction of his concept of the *negative* was Winnicott—in particular, the Winnicott of *Playing and Reality*. The paper is an illustration of how Green was inspired by these themes of absence, loss, and transitional phenomena. Incidentally, this is another rare glimpse of actual clinical data in Green's work—the first and the fifth lectures are the only two papers in this collection where you will find clinical vignettes. In this fifth paper Green tells us of a patient he treated who had been seen by Winnicott himself. She had been told that Dr Green was "a kind of French Winnicott".

After starting work with this patient under difficult geographical circumstances, Green realized that this was the patient to whom Winnicott refers in the final section of his seminal paper, "Transitional Objects and Transitional Phenomena" (1971). Winnicott's clinical example is an illustration of the patient's inability

EDITOR'S FOREWORD xv

to keep the Other in mind. For this patient the analyst who was *not* there felt more real than the analyst who *was* there. This is wholly relevant to a passage in Winnicott's paper, "The Location of Cultural Experience" (Chapter 7 of *Playing and Reality*), where he vividly describes the process of internalization for the infant in relation to the crucial factor of the mother's timing:

> The feeling of the mother's existence lasts x minutes. If the mother is away more than x minutes, then the imago fades, and along with this the baby's capacity to use the symbol of the union ceases. The baby is distressed, but this distress is soon mended because the mother returns in x + y minutes. In x + y minutes the baby has not become altered. But in x + y + z minutes the mother's return does not mend the baby's altered state. Trauma implies that the baby has experienced a break in life's continuity, so that primitive defenses now become organized to defend against a repetition of "unthinkable anxiety" or a return of the acute confusional state that belongs to disintegration of nascent ego structure. [1971b, p. 97]

Green explores and discusses how Winnicott intuits the nature of absence and its impact on the infant's inability to internalize a reliable object. These are the themes that are intrinsically part of his concept of the *negative*.

The third and fourth lectures

"This is the crux of the matter: that one day this paradise has to come to an end, that two in one becomes two who are kept apart, and this is why a third is needed." [p. 63]

Nina Farhi invited André Green twice more: in 1991, when he presented a lecture entitled "On Thirdness"; and again in 1996, for the Centenary Celebrations of Winnicott's work.

If you read the papers here in order of appearance, you will discern how the themes elaborate and develop into the subject of thirdness in the paper of this title. This is where André Green brings together the thought of Charles Sanders Peirce, a nineteenth-century semiotician (semiotics = the study of signs) with that of Freud and Winnicott and in doing so creates a new psychoanalytic object—thirdness. The multidimensional quality and complexity of this paper conveys the very essence of thirdness—symbolization and the art of thinking.

I was also reminded of Winnicott's posthumously published paper, "The Use of an Object in the Context of Moses and Monotheism" (1969) in *Psycho-Analytic Explorations* (1989), where he writes:

> It is easy to make the assumption that because the mother starts as a part object or as a conglomeration of part objects the father comes into ego-grasp in the same way. But I suggest that in a favourable case the father starts off whole (i.e.: as father, not as mother surrogate) and later becomes endowed with a significant part object, that he starts off as an integrate in the ego's organization and in the mental conceptualization of the baby. [p. 243]

Winnicott never denied the importance of the third for the baby's healthy development, but perhaps it is easy to forget this when, as he confessed, he did so much wish to speak to mothers. But reading this posthumously published paper, it is clear that Winnicott's thinking towards the end of his life is in line with Green's emphasis—namely, that the father in the mother's mind (the reality of the sexual union) is the whole father that will be felt by the baby at the beginning. And for Green it is this fact that constitutes the basis of mental health.

In 1996 André Green presented his paper, "The Posthumous Winnicott—On *Human Nature*", as part of *Squiggle's* Winnicott Centenary Celebrations. On that occasion we were treated again, and this time with Green's observations and reflections on Winnicott's profound contribution to psychoanalysis as outlined in his posthumously published book, *Human Nature* (1988). Green says of this book that it is "a transitional writing between the unsaid and the published" ... "a book ... that both is and is not the text" ... "fragments of an unfinished symphony" (pp. 69, 70). He begins this paper by commenting on two conclusions that he came to after reading *Human Nature*. The first was "how Donald W. Winnicott's recapitulation was in continuation with Freud's work"—that he "did not break off with Freud but rather completed his work" (p. 70). The second was how much of an independent thinker

Winnicott was. "He was the true leader of the independent stream in the British Psycho-Analytical Society" (p. 70). Like the fifth paper in this collection, this fourth paper is a true celebration of Winnicott's thought.

Although André Green has published 14 books and over 200 articles, until recently the only book in English that was well known to the analytic community had been the collection (as mentioned above) *On Private Madness* (1986). Those of you familiar with that work will recognize many of the themes presented in these papers reiterated here. The central theme of exclusion from the primal scene and its influence on borderline defences in the "*dead mother complex*" will be seen in "Experience and Thinking in Analytic Practice"; the multi-layering of object–subject relationships and their impact on the oedipal constellation in "Object(s) and Subject"; and the quintessential Greenian elaboration of Freud and Winnicott—tertiary processes, symbolization, transitional phenomena, and the role of the third—in "On Thirdness".

Squiggle *celebrating the work of André Green*

On 22 November 1998, the Foundation held a day's conference in celebration of André Green's work. Michael Parsons and Juliet Mitchell talked in the morning, and Gregorio Kohon introduced André Green in the afternoon, before Green himself extemporized on the papers of the morning. It was an excellent and memorable conference.[2]

The last year of the century brought more English translations of Green's work: *The Dead Mother—The Work of André Green*, edited by Gregorio Kohon (1999)—a collection of papers by eminent analysts in celebration of Green's work, one of which is the paper

---

[2]The conference "Celebrating the Work of André Green" was held at the Brunei Gallery on 22 November 1998. Details of the day can be obtained from the *Squiggle* Foundation, 33 Amberley Road, London N13 4BH, Tel. 020 8882 9744.

presented by Michael Parsons, as mentioned above—and *The Fabric of Affect in the Psychoanalytic Discourse* (1999a). This latter book had originally been published in 1973! In addition, *The Work of the Negative*, originally published in 1993, has also now been published in English (1999b). Increasingly, then, the Anglo-Saxon world will have access to the thinking of André Green. That this monograph will contribute to the corpus of Dr Green's work is a great honour and very much in line with *Squiggle's* primary aim—to disseminate the work and tradition of D. W. Winnicott.

ANDRÉ GREEN
at The *Squiggle* Foundation

André Green

ONE

Experience and thinking in analytic practice

After I had decided on the title of this lecture, I wondered why I had chosen it. I think that it was because I would have to speak to this particular audience, and for me, of course, The *Squiggle* Foundation is associated with Winnicott. Winnicott's work, and what I know about him through the people who knew him personally, is probably best summarized with the two terms from my title: how to match *experience* in analytic work—without which there cannot be any kind of work in the setting—and *thinking*, a matter on which Winnicott has been much more discreet.

Winnicott was a great thinker—we are all aware of that—but perhaps he was something of a *spontaneous* thinker. I mean that *thinking* for him was deeply bound up with *experience*. So, even if his work gives us a lot to think about, he does not provide a true theory of thinking, such as we find, for instance, in Bion's work—which, for me, is very close to Winnicott's. What is certain is that

---

This *Squiggle* Public Lecture was given on 3 March 1987 at Primrose Hill Community Centre, North London.

as analysts we are engaged in an experience with the patient, and, while the meaning of what happens in this experience may be obscure to us, we are still able to feel the experience, to talk about it, even though the meaning of what is going on eludes us.

What we can say is that the experience is an *actualization*. I prefer this term to any other because I think that other words can be misleading. There have been discussions in psychoanalysis as to whether the psychoanalytic experience is a repetition of the past, or a creation—that is, a thing that is entirely new and is created by the analytic situation, and that does not and could not exist apart from the situation (Freud, 1937d). So in order not to take sides in this debate, I prefer to call it an *actualization*, and in this *actualization* the experience has to do with the historical nature of man. What I mean here is that now that we have moved on a bit from Freud's statement on repetition—we are all aware that it is not enough to speak of the analytic experience in terms of recovering memories, or reliving memories from infantile amnesia—what goes on in this experience still has to do with the historical process. What goes on between these two partners, analyst and analysand, is a historical process in that it deals with the way in which history is constituted in a person: how it works, how it becomes effective. So, rather than speaking of recovering memories, one has the feeling at certain moments within the analytic relationship that one is witnessing something historical, just as when you have been witnessing certain kinds of events you have the feeling that something historical is going on in the present.

As far as psychoanalysis is concerned, the historical is a very difficult notion to handle. Presently much psychoanalytic work goes on with children, as well as other kinds of infant research, and I want to make it clear that this is very different from what I call the historical perspective, as far as the psyche is concerned. Because, for the psyche, the historical could be defined as a combination of:

—what has happened,
—what has not happened,
—what could have happened,
—what has happened to someone else but not to me,

—what could not have happened,

—and finally—to summarize all these alternatives about what has happened—a statement that one would not have even dreamed of as a representation of what really happened.

This is what I mean by the historical perspective, and this is what we are experiencing in the analytic situation. My reference to the dream was an allusion to what I call the *negative*, and in this lecture I will try to elucidate the relationship between *thinking* and the *negative*. Here the dream appears as the *negative* of the event. Of course, there are basic psychoanalytic concepts about the dream, and about the relationship between the dream and wish-fulfilment. What I would like to deal with first is the relationship between a dream and the wish-fulfilment as an example of both the *negative* and of thinking.

In relation to reality, it is not just (even if you take the simplest formulation about the dream) that the dream is an attempt to realize a wish. We can view it not only in terms of the satisfaction of conquering an obstacle in the dream, which it has not been possible to overcome in reality, but also that the dream—as an example of the *negative*—introduces us to the idea that the *negative* is a work, not a state. For instance, still considering this simplest example, the dream satisfies itself not only by virtue of some sort of reward attached to the wish-fulfilment, but also by virtue of some censorship. So, the fact that censorship is allowed to take place—censorship that existed in waking life and is still present in the dream—makes us understand certain things about the *negative*. It is the by-product of the maintenance of something that cannot receive any kind of realization and is a way of realizing it in a different manner, in a different organization, in a different form, in a different type of experience of reality. But here, the *negative* has another interest for us: more than reality, the *negative* gives us a view of the structure and organization of the mind. When one is engaged in the experience (with all the affective involvement with which the experience is loaded), one does not see, and one is not able to be aware of, how the reality of the experience, and the reality that serves as the setting for the experience, is organized. It is only through the dream that one can have an idea of the elements and the factors that play a role in the organization of experience and that cannot be understood immediately or directly, but only in the reverse, within the transformed situation that dreams enable us to see. So, the *negative* here is not only the reverse of the positive in the sense that it frees us from the limitation of the positive, but also in that it reveals what cannot be seen in the positive experience.

The analytic situation has itself been compared to a dream, and I said earlier that it was an actualization—but an actualization of what? This is a question that we cannot answer, or, rather, that we can only answer by referring to the *negative*. I can give at least two pointers, in terms of what is activated in the analytic experience— an experience that brings two partners into contact who are separated by differences in their functioning. The actualization is about something that refers to somewhere else, to some other space, and to some other time. Everything in the analytic situation is very highly loaded by this actualization and seems to be profoundly present. It gives a sensation of intensity and closeness that is, of course, not comparable to any other type of relationship, in terms of its type of dialogue. However, this is a dialogue that seems and feels so close that it almost resembles a sexual relationship more than a dialogue. There is no sexual contact, though, so despite that very strong impression of presentness, what goes on is always in the end related to another place and another time. Here, I am of course referring to the past, but that is not as simple a statement as it looks. We are not talking of a narrowly historical past, and we are not talking about the present time of the relationship: the other place and time can also be the future, or could be a fantasy.

One of the meanings of the *negative* is that one can only become aware of it after having had an experience of the *negative* and recognized it as such. For instance, the awareness of it is in the analytic encounter after a good interpretation has been given. One has the feeling of having achieved something—as if one has finally brought home and found shelter for something—some wandering piece of mind. It is then that you become aware that, before the interpretation, it was not there. Nothing has changed: the patient was talking, you were listening, and after the good interpretation has happened you realize that something was absent and you understand why it could not have been there before.

The place of the *negative* in current psychoanalytic theory is much more important than one might have guessed. For instance, if we take Freud's basic concept of hallucinatory wish-fulfilment, which is considered as the cell and matrix of the mind, the necessary condition for this happening is, of course, the *absence* of the breast. When, later in his career, Freud had considered the different natures of the dream from that of hallucination, he came to the conclusion that in fact there were no differences that could be used to draw an absolute distinction between them. However, he added in one footnote that every positive hallucination had to be preceded by a negative hallucination (Freud, 1917d [1915]). Now, that means, of course, that this creation of the mind always depends on a state of absence: either something should be there and is not, or is there and should not be.

These basic ideas, which are not quite clearly developed in Freud's work, are also found in the writings of other thinkers. For instance, Bion gives the very important distinction between the nothing and the no-thing—the fact that in order to build up a theory of thinking, it is an absolute necessity to start from the absence of the breast. Essentially it is the *tolerance* of the absence of the breast that is necessary for the building-up of the thought processes. This "no-breast" (this no-thing) is quite different from that other, almost identical word, "nothing". There must be some state that is *between* absolute loss and excessive presence, some state of tolerance of the mind to which we are accustomed in terms of fantasy or in terms of representation. To me, either fantasy or representation are ways of filling up this gap which denotes a state of suspended experience. This brings us to Winnicott, who, I believe, was very aware of this phenomenon. The notion of potential space is one of the most striking examples of how Winnicott thought about the problem of the *negative* without really labelling it or pinning it down precisely. When you extend the notion of the negative, you find yourself dealing with the realm of virtuality, absence, possibility, and potentiality. Of course, this is one of the meanings of the negative, the sense in which it opens up the possibility of the work of the negative. To some extent, this limits the boundlessness of the negative, giving it form, content, and, as it were, a terrain. An inherently restless attitude of mind opens up the potential for the *work of the negative*.

Here we encounter a particular problem: we use the word "negative" also to refer to that which is destructive. This problem is, I believe, not only terminological, but also semantic. It is no accident that language uses the same term to designate the negative, referring to a photographic negative. In this sense, one is thinking about the way in which a piece of reality, or an experience, can be inverted. With this way of seeing things, you may come to perceive aspects of the organization of an experience which escaped you when looking at the "positive" experience. For instance, Freud describes a turning-around upon the subject's own self (or the reversal) into its opposite, as the mechanism that occurs before the outcome and achievement of repression. I think it is very striking that he gave an immense role to the negative, not only as something that one wants to get rid of, or wants to push as far as possible from one's own consciousness, but also, in fact, to show that it has the possibility of reverting into the opposite, or turning into oneself something that was previously directed at the object.

In his paper "Negation" (1925h), Freud writes: "With the help of the symbol of negation, thinking frees itself from the restrictions of repression" (p. 236). This is the part of the sentence that is usually quoted, but Freud adds, "and enriches itself with material that is indispensable for its proper functioning" (p. 236). He does not elaborate his hypothesis. According to the text, it is reasonable to suppose that Freud is alluding to the relationship between the thing-presentations—specific to the unconscious, where no negation takes place—and word-presentations, which include the use of negation. Thinking, therefore, depends on the relationship between thing-presentations and word-presentations. We then have to make it clear what qualities the representational system, beyond the difference between the two types of representations, have to possess in order to facilitate the transformation from one to the other. It could be that the answer lies in the possibility that the wish is given the status of a realization in the mind and is not just a reproduction of the result of a perception. We would have to turn to an extension of the relationship between "thing" and "word" and consider the condition in which a wish can be treated as "fulfillable". The "roots" of thinking have to be extended to a wider concept of representation in the psychic world of what arises in the body, and the response that is given to what the body requires, that is registered through the traces left by objects that stand ultimately in the external world and that are called upon in the first instance. Representation, therefore, in psychoanalytic experience, has a much more extended meaning than in the philosophical tradition. It would have to deal less with a simple static condition than be viewed as a process that takes place at a crossroads, always towards achieving some sort of satisfaction (if not in reality, then in the mind), till finally the object takes over.

In my view, Freud sees negation as essential to thinking—not only in terms of the secondary processes, where of course the distinction between I and not-I is important, but I think also in the whole range of the mind, even in its more primitive forms. Of course, I think that Freud made a considerable advancement when he postulated this idea that was—and still is—absolutely revolutionary: that is, when he gave precedence to the judgement of attribution over the judgement of existence. First you attribute a quality—good or bad—and then you have to decide whether a thing exists or not. We still have to ponder on the complete reversal of thinking that this entails. I think the fact that his (1925h) paper ends by discussing the relationship between negation and what Freud calls the destructive impulses, or the death instinct, offers many possibilities for research and thinking in psychoanalysis.

In the analytic situation, the thing that exists or does not exist (as one may decide from one's own perceptions) is related not only to the good and the bad, but also to the hidden and the apparent. With some patients who are difficult to handle and to analyse, we are often ill at ease with this destructiveness. This is because, although we can accept that they are using us as an object on which they can act out in their mind their destructive impulses, at the same time the fact is that what they are destroying is largely insight in the analytic situation—that is, the destruction of a mind that would otherwise be shared by the two people in this encounter. One has to ask oneself, what are the unconscious dynamics that lie behind that type of destructive action? I think that in terms of the negative, we can see how it takes an unconscious form. These patients unknowingly conceal a kind of unconscious postulate, which is: "What I have to hide is related to what is hidden by the other." This happens if the other, the analyst as an object, appears to the patient as wishing to deny his ability to relate to any third party outside the analytic situation. This is the reversal of a normal envious situation: it is not the subject who envies the analyst; it is the analyst who is supposed to envy the analysand's potential to relate to somebody outside the analytic situation. This envy is sustained by the fact that what has to remain hidden, in this relationship to the object, is that the partner, the object, the analyst, has the capacity to relate to a third person.

I shall now report a case that will, I hope, bring together some of the ideas that I have been discussing. The patient is a woman who is now in her thirties. She was referred to me after several suicide attempts and hospitalizations because of the prolonged comas after these attempts. There had been a lot of acting-out during an earlier period of therapy with a colleague of mine. This seems to have been a mutually seductive relationship in which she wanted to force him to go to bed with her. She threatened suicide and finally made a suicidal attempt on the stairwell just in front of his door. Finally, this relationship was interrupted, and I'm mentioning this because it is one circumstance in which the father seemed to really act in a way that the child wanted him to—that is, the action of stopping the relationship.

She had lived for part of her childhood in Africa, and she related (after the beginning of her treatment with me, which was face-to-face) that at the age of six she had been sexually seduced by an African servant who was called the "boy". She denounced the servant after several such experiences and was extremely surprised when he was sent to jail. This, of course, raised an enormous amount of unconscious guilt, because she also liked him. To some extent this could explain all the hospitalizations—in which of course she found herself in some sort of jail, like the "boy". The feelings associated with her memories of childhood carry an immense weight of sadness and solitude.

When the treatment started four years ago, a lot of acting-out was initially present. In the sessions, she would stand up and walk around saying that she felt like breaking all the furniture or pushing down all the books from the shelves. She even once took hold of me by my jacket and was strong enough to make me stand up: she wanted to put me on the couch. Fortunately—I don't quite know how—it just so happened that she fell onto the couch, which, importantly, neither of us was using. She would, of course, make all sorts of things happen in the external world to express her anxiety and to worry me. For instance, once she was locked in a cinema, hiding after the last performance, and then at three o'clock in the morning she made a lot of noise so that people came and freed her. At a certain point during the treatment she also had what I assumed was probably a psychotic episode. I felt that she was the sort of person who had to hide the psychotic aspects of herself so as to try to look normal. During the sessions at this time, she would say that she did not want to listen to anything I had to say, though she came to the sessions regularly, never missing one. Once, in a state probably resulting from a split-off part of the personality, she said: "Dr Green: my father and myself we fuck you off in the arse." It was obviously a reversal of her traumatic childhood experience that she wanted me to experience in her place. But the anxiety that was expressed was probably due to the fact that she brought the father into the picture. This could indicate, at the very least, her wish to get something from him, which she thought would give her some kind of potency, but because of the anger such a potency did not reassure her, but instead worried her, because the sense of guilt transformed it and thus it became only destructive. Some time later, she completely lost her memory of having said this. She was also prone to fits of depersonalization, in which states she perhaps found something of use, because it forced her awareness of herself. This patient did not know the meaning of the word anxiety when she came to me—during her actings-out and her impulses to break the furniture, I would stress the state of anxiety that she was communicating, and she would say that she did not understand what I was talking about. This, too, is a manifestation of the negative, and it took her years before she recognized her anxiety states.

The interesting thing—and the reason that I'm talking about this patient—is to note what has happened, now that she has improved a lot, and is behaving—at least apparently—like any other normal person. At present the analytic work is the most difficult for her and for me, and it is now that we can witness what I would call all the potency of the negative. Of course one can say, well, what you mean is denial, and in a sense, yes, that is what I'm saying. But denial is an anti-expression if you do not link it up with the whole structure of the mind and all that goes with it, all the manifestations of the negative and all the ramifications of how one can live by denying one's internal world through the distortion of experiences. What I'm going to discuss is a recent sequence of events; as I said, at the present moment she is functioning fairly well. She is living all by herself, she can bear solitude, she has her own flat, she has a job, she sees friends from time to time, but she has no relationship with anyone else except me. Of course she sees friends, but she has no major relationship except with her parents, whom she visits most weekends; apart from this, there is no meaningful and significant person in her life except myself.

Now we are coming to the point of the treatment where she has arrived at the following rationalization: "Well, now I realize that things are very simple. I have totally failed and missed out on my relationship with my father because my father is aloof, and distant." In the family, too, this is the accepted version, and the parental couple is united on a very strange level with the patient, almost like accomplices. It also happens that the patient's mother is an illegitimate child and has hardly seen her father. In addition, the father of the patient had a mother who was ill with tuberculosis, which prevented him from establishing any kind of closeness with her. The patient's mother is always complaining about the patient's father, that he is like a child who does not take care of the children as a father should, and so on. Personally, I was quite sure that this was the situation, but that this was not the most significant thing about the figure of the father in the patient's inner world. Many things suggested that the father, because of his aloofness and his distance, was terrifying and dreadfully feared by her.

Once she told me about a game she remembered playing when she was a child, but that she had no idea why it was so pleasant for her. She said that she remembered that when she was a little girl and they were living in a flat in France rather than in Africa, at a certain time of the day her brother and sister would be having a bath together. Just near the bathroom was the kitchen, where their mother would be preparing the dinner. She said: "Well, I don't know why I didn't have my bath with my brother and sister." Without me asking anything, she said that she did not remember having played any sexual games, and one explanation could be that she did not bathe with her siblings. But the game was that she went from the bathroom, just glanced at her mother preparing the dinner, went past the bathroom, ran down the corridor, stopped, came back, going past the bathroom again, looked at her mother, and then repeated the sequence. At the end of the corridor which she ran down was the parents' bedroom. She interpreted this game by saying that she probably took pleasure in it because of feeling reassured that her mother was still there in the kitchen preparing the dinner, and that she was relieved because she was not in Africa, which was associated with all the memories about the sexual abuse. My interpretation was that the pleasure was linked to the fantasy that the mother could disappear during her running and that she might find herself alone in the parents' bedroom with her father, and that she had to reassure herself that this had not happened. Her answer was that this was a stupid suggestion: "My father never existed for me—he paid no attention to my presence. My mother always told us that he wouldn't notice if we weren't there, that you'd have to wait three or four days before he notices anything." So, she said, I was totally wrong in what I had said.

Two days after this, she brought a dream in which she saw her father alone in the bathroom holding a tool which in French we call *clef anglaise* ["English key"]—in fact, it is an adjustable spanner. There was a condensation between the father's tool and the consonance of my name. There was some history associated with this *clef anglaise*: she had had to repair her own motorcycle and had borrowed this tool, which was very precious to her father, who had agreed to lend it to her. She used it, and she lost it. Of course, the presence of the father in the bathroom was an allusion to her game because that was where the brother and sister had been, possibly involved in some sexual contact. Again, we find the desire to keep the father's tool and the sense of guilt. She did not give it back, which made her father angry. And so, she observed, it was strange, because it completely contradicted her assertion that her father did not exist for her and because it reminded her of the game. The negative element of the game appeared in the dream; the presence of the father who was supposed not to be there anyway, and who was negatively supposed to be in the parents' empty bedroom at the end of the corridor which she was on her way to.

Now I want to give a bit of material to do with the handling of the negative in the transference. Once she had a session at the beginning of the afternoon, and as I had to go and have lunch outside, we met, coincidentally, in the street at the entrance of my house and so took the lift together. I left her in the waiting-room, and, as I had two or three minutes before the start of the session, I went to my kitchen and ate a bit of chocolate. When I opened the door of the waiting-room to let her into the consulting-room, her first sentence was, "Did you eat some chocolate?" Now, as you may know, French analysts do not answer questions, so I did not say anything about whether or not I had eaten chocolate. During the session I understood her question as an expression of how she needed to, not quite control me, but at least to know exactly what I was doing in her absence in that very short space of time. It was a period when I had announced my dates for the Easter holiday, and often at such times—though less now—she would speak about an outburst of love for the former analyst. That analysis is now twelve years ago, though she had met him again last summer.

When I interpreted the reason why she had that outburst of love, I suggested that I was not as manageable as he had been: that he had always been available, that she could telephone him at any time of the day or night, and that, of course, created the illusion that there had been nobody between them, no third person of any sort. She had the feeling that she would not have to be confronted by any obstacle between them, and that was what she seemed to find pleasant in evoking that situation. When she talked about this love for the other analyst again, it was easy to show how this was meant to make me jealous, so that she did not have to feel jealous at the thought of my departure with someone else. At the subsequent session—and this is the point that I want to discuss—she came and said that she had not been able to sleep. She suffered from insomnia, and she said that she could not sleep any more; she had not taken any pills for a while, but now, she said, she needed to because things had gone so badly between us. She then spoke of her father's tantrums, and she said that the fear I had suggested that she had of me must surely be linked with her father, who appeared to her as a kind of god threatening her with thunder and storm. Then she mentioned a lunch she had with a woman who was a friend of her parents, and who had submitted some stories to be broadcasted, which had been accepted. (My patient had made a similar attempt a few months earlier and had failed at the last stage of assessment, having received favourable comments up until then). Broadcasting is significant because her father works in that field, and both she and her father write. During the lunch, she said, the woman told her her opinion about her stories. She went on to say—and it was difficult to know whether this was the judgement of the friend or of herself—that they were not stories, that she was not creative or intellectual, and that she had no artistic gifts. There was a strong feeling, at least, that this assessment derived from what the woman had said. Her reaction was to say that it did not matter to her that much, and, because a lot of hatred had been mentioned about her parents and about my breaks, I said, "No, the matter isn't serious. What would be serious is if you weren't able to recreate me when I had gone, in one way or another." Of course, I was aware how much she must have felt offended by this criticism, but I supposed that the worst thing in it was the extent to which she was out of touch with her need to reshape her inner experience, in a way that could be shown to others.

At that point, I was reminded of a very strong emotional reaction that she'd had, regarding a picture of herself as a small child. She had described it in two ways: in the first interpretation, she said that it showed her mother clinging to her, holding her feet, and preventing her from running to go and play on the beach; and she thought that she was more mature in that picture than her own parents. But then she looked again at the picture and said that the reason it impressed her so much was how solitary and sad she felt, while, she said, her parents were laughing all the time in her presence. So I made the interpretation that probably she reacted to my holidays so strongly not only because I was away and unavailable, but also because I too was laughing all the time with somebody else about her loneliness. I said that she felt deprived of that because probably if she could laugh like me, that would give her an immense power, the sort of power to impose silence, as the father did in his temper tantrums. Her response was that she did not understand.

To come back to my main subject, Freud at the end of his paper on "Negation" (1925h) says that when the patient answers an interpretation by saying "I didn't think that", or "I didn't ever think of that", this is the strongest evidence of the uncovering of the unconscious. The *work of the negative* is what is taking place when someone has the feeling of never having thought something, and yet clues can be given that the thought can be facilitated in them. But when a patient says, "I don't understand", this is the negative statement of "I never thought of that", and it is a destructive statement, although appearing innocuous, because it means that the patient does not grasp anything in terms of contact, is unable to make any link with the interpretation, and therefore cannot engender the unknown thought. It is the generation of the unknown thought that is important, and its denial is the negative as destructive, rather than the negative as facilitating the unknown.

I think that to say "I don't understand" in English is more revealing than if one used the French word, "*comprendre*". "*Comprendre*" gives the sense of putting ideas or thoughts together, but the English word is much better because it evokes for me one of the most interesting and most obscure concepts of psychoanalysis, which is cathexis. What we call the "object relationship" is in fact a kind of stream, which is the pre-requirement to any process of transformation to representations or to thought, just as having ground under your feet is a prerequisite to being able to stand.

So I took the "I don't understand", and I said: "Now you're taking what has been said—that you're not creative, intellectual, nor artistically gifted—to mean that you have no reason to share anything with me, and you can't come close to me." While talking, I was aware of a quality of silence that was not the usual one. When I finished, the patient said to me, "While you were talking, I closed my eyes and listened to what you were saying. I listened to the sound of your voice, and also to your words, but particularly to your voice. I pictured in my mind your animated face, and I felt very close to you." This is banal. She added ". . . and all because of the piece of chocolate of yesterday". I said: "You wanted to be that chocolate, so that I would eat you." She said: "Oh yes, of course. For instance, when I meet someone who has a good smell or a perfume, I want to be that perfume in order to be part of the person who is wearing it."

This was an example of what I mean by the *work of the negative*, and of the two aspects of the negative. On the one hand, there is what happens during absence, the destructive aspects, the denial of envy, the denial of the desire to be linked up with the third party, which is in another place and another time. This has to be brought back home and thus creates not so much the movement of introjection, but more importantly the movement that is created inside the subject and leaves the subject in order to go towards some object. In calling this, as we do, "object relationship", we do not take sufficient account of this movement outwards and towards not only objects, but also the world; and it is this that is the other aspect of the negative. It is only if the patient can experience that feeling of movement in the session that I think he will be able to continue moving and working outside the session in the world. That is why I said, at the beginning of the lecture, that I had a feeling that psychoanalysis has to do with history and with the historical nature of man, not only in terms of recovering the past, but also of making the present and being in the present as a historical being, through a process during which progressing towards the object mobilizes all the transformations of the past that are relevant to the present situation and finds new room for the expectations that have not found a way to link themselves with the transformations, either because of the anxieties associated with them, or because of the impossibility of avoiding destruction because of the fear that arises in the mind of damaging the objects towards which the drives are directed.

TWO

Object(s) and subject

The more I work, read, and think in psychoanalysis, the more I become aware of a phenomenon that every analyst who tries to write is exposed to. While communicating about our work, we use the language of secondary processes in order to convey an unknown experience, which we think of as primary processes, or the experience of psychic reality or of the unconscious. We do not know this realm very well, and, as time goes by and as our psychoanalytic experience increases, we are not necessarily led to find an appropriate language for this task. Indeed, the passing of time has another, quite opposite, effect. It is this: the more one looks at psychoanalytic theory, the more one sees that it resembles the language of secondary processes, and perhaps it diverges from the essence of psychoanalytic experience. This is a tendency in modern psychoanalysis and can make psychoanalysis look rather like phenomenology—that is, what is conveyed from psychoanalytic experience and the inner world is a

---

This *Squiggle* Public Lecture was given on 2 June 1990 at Primrose Hill Community Centre, North London.

way of restating experience in descriptive terms. My feeling, as I say, is that this tendency is closer to introspection than to true psychoanalytic thinking.

One example of this is the present conception of theory in terms of self and object. This formulation is a fairly recent one, and I am not going to retrace all the steps that led from the ego to the self. What I would like to say is that on the one hand we have a theory about "object relations" that perhaps causes us some difficulties in French that do not occur in English. "Object relations" is translated in French as *relation d'objet*, or by the adjective, as in *relation objectale*. When you say *objectal* in French, it is the opposite of *objectif*—that is, objective. In English you do not have that problem, because "object relations" covers the whole field. Speaking of internal objects and external objects, it seems enough to underline that the world of objects is a world that contains many aspects. For instance, when you think of the opposite, nobody ever talks of "subject relations".[1] There is a concept in Winnicott of egorelatedness, but I do not think that this is equivalent to anything that might be called "subject relations".[2]

It is interesting to see that in English psychoanalytic literature the word "subject" is not used very much. The concepts of "ego" and "self" are used, but there are two other concepts that are not used in English, whilst being prominent in French psychoanalytic writing. In France, we speak of *le soi* [the self] just as you do, as distinct from the ego, and we also refer to *le sujet* as the subject, which is not a concept that you seem to use. My feeling is that the more one talks of the "self", the more one goes in a direction that is, I feel, dangerous, because it is mainly descriptive, and this is misleading. The emphasis that is placed on the experience of the self tends to give an account of that experience in phenomenological terms—that is, in conscious terms. As I have said, my concern is, what then becomes of the unconscious? Therefore, what I have in mind is that there is an entire set of descriptions with probably very different features which one could call a "subject

---

[1] But Winnicott (1963) does talk of subjective objects.
[2] Coincidentally, Christopher Bollas talks about subject relations in *Forces of Destiny* (1989, p. 108). Dr Green had written this paper before the publication of that book.

relationship". It would encompass a whole series, including the "ego", the "I", the "self", and the "subject", as different and distinct features. As far as I'm concerned, I choose from these two terms—the "ego" and the "subject"—because I find them more useful and more appropriate than the notion of "self", which loses any specificity. The "self" has always had a conscious connotation; by contrast, I use "ego" in Freud's sense, and not in the everyday one, as an agency defined by its relationship to the two others: the id and the superego.

At this point, I have run into the problems that inevitably arise when one writes an essay in French and has to deliver it in English. I was about to say, "*Le Moi se prend pour moi*", and if I translated that, it would be "The ego mistakes itself for me." What does that mean? It means that the ego, which is really one part of me, cannot avoid pretending that it is the whole of myself, the total personality—in other words, thinks, falsely, that it is me. I think that it was an extraordinary theoretical leap when Freud began to think of the ego as one agency of the personality, and not as its totality—a meaning in which he sometimes indulged before 1923—which, by definition, cannot be grasped independently. As he wrote in "The Dependent Relationships of the Ego" (Chapter V of *The Ego and the Id* [1923b]), it is one of the functions of the ego to be attacked, contested, and challenged by the other agencies of the personality.

This is why, instead of speaking of the "self", I prefer the term "subject". As we will see shortly, the idea of "self" misleads us, because it gives us the impression that we can encompass the whole of what we are—which I think, from the psychoanalytic perspective, is not possible. One justification for using the concept of "self" is that we have found more and more patients who suffer from identity disorders, where such a concept seems more appropriate. The idea of the "self" is centred by the notion of unity. This is supposed to be the achievement of harmonious development. If one forgets that this harmony is essentially developed out of tolerable conflicts between the conscious and the unconscious, this could be an illusion as well as a denial of the presence of the unconscious. We can speak of tensions that compromise solutions and allow the ego to go on, but we cannot speak of a totally pacified system. The sense of identity can only exist if it is regularly challenged, without of course the threat of a breakdown, which will affect not only the ego but the whole structure of internal relationships and relationships to the object. The best a person can achieve is being two, never one—a conscious and an unconscious—let alone the possibility of further splitting. People who suffer from identity disorders are in a far worse position than this because they are split into minute parts. This is a theoretical sleight-of-hand that can mislead us into thinking of the "self" as a unity.

I think that using the concept of the "subject" does not have the same pitfalls. One of the senses of "subject" is the linguistic one. One knows from grammar that one cannot dissociate the subject from the object, the verb, and the complement; the subject is only part of an entity—the sentence—but it is mainly related to the action—namely, the verb. And I think that the sentence is a much more fruitful model, considering (for instance) the case where one does not just have a simple subject-and-object relationship, but instead a relationship between subject and object that also concerns a third person. To my mind, the whole of psychic structure is based on "thirdness" (but this is another topic for another lecture). In this last view we see that just as for the "ego", the "subject" is defined by its relationship to other entities. At least, in language, the relationships are all established on the homogeneity conferred by language. The situation is different when we ask how such a unity could be achieved in an apparatus whose parts are so different, not only in their functions, but also in the different material that is characteristic of each agency (drives, representations, perceptions, ideals, etc.), not to say anything about the way each type links together and connects with the others.

The unconscious subject is something that is very difficult to conceive of. As far as the unconscious is concerned, I do not think that we can speak in terms of the unconscious subject as something covering the whole experience of the self. I shall try to present some of the features that make the distinction between the well-known functions of the ego and those that are carried by the subject. It was Lacan who took the initiative of promoting this idea. He mainly emphasized two aspects. The subject was conceived in relation to the signifier. This view of the subject, through dealing with language, was not to be confused with the grammatical subject. It leaned on the differentiation, classical in linguistics, between the subject within the proposition and the subject that spells out the proposition (*sujet de l'énoncé, sujet de l'énonciation*). The main idea, which was very evocative for Lacan, was the splitting it involved. He was relying on Freud's last paper, "The Splitting of the Ego in the Process of Defence" (1940e [1938]). What was said about the ego was transposed to the subject. It was fundamentally split, in normality as in pathology, in such a way that it could never achieve its unity. Though it was Freud's discovery, Lacan found that it could support his idea of a radical alienation, which, he stated, was an alienation of the subject from his own speech. In the very attempt of communicating, the production of one's speech would betray the splitting. Was it really from one's own speech that the subject was alienated? In the past, Lacan defended the idea—after Hegel—that it was desire that decentred the subject and how the alienation occurred—meaning that his feelings and his desire were outside the realm of his ego. Now, it was as if he had killed two birds with one stone, equating speech and desire. The reason for this amalgam is that the manifestation of the subject's desire had to go through his passionate declaration. Here Lacan was thinking of the transference in the analytic situation. He finally postulated the idea of a subject as the agent of the combination of the signifiers that were operating behind the scenes in the unconscious through the symbolic, which will betray themselves in the communication with the other (the unconscious) and the other (the object of desire).

In my view, this concept of the subject is too narrowly tied to language. I would prefer to extend it to the wider sphere of representation. The main relationship of the subject is to what may be called "representance"—that is, the multiple ways in which the basic forms of messages are represented, reproduced, and transformed trying to articulate (more or less) compatible expressions, which in turn help their transmission from one type to another, according to the tensions, censorship, achievements, emergencies that are taking place in the psychic apparatus. It should be clear that this concept has nothing to do with any synthetic function of the ego, as synthesis is not the aim; rather, it is in order to maintain the specificity of each type, because each type has its own way of communicating the work it performs in its specific location and in an opposite direction. The different types also have to convey their answers to the question they have had to respond to. The system is not guided by adaptation, but by the way conflict is treated in the mind, and it does not so much allow for a solution as having to accept the impossibility of arriving at an unequivocal answer. It would also be misleading to understand this function of representance as being related to any kind of self observation, because of the absence of the system that would be able to meld the different forms of a representation into a united reading of communication. Language is a vector; the direction, followed by its representations, leaves behind much of what should be communicated—like affects—but is not. The ego-subject is the seat of tertiary processes, processes that I have proposed to define as linking the products of primary and secondary processes. This agency, associating ego and subject, can acquire self-reference, but this is probably under the influence of the part that is attached to the ego. As far as the subject is concerned, we can underline that having to confront the different systems of representation implies that it cannot be located in only one of the traditional agencies. Facing the impossibility of the ego imposing its solutions on the other agencies, the representational subject helps it to deal with mediations, which (still without being in a position to master them) he will communicate to the messengers they become, in order to search for compromises.

Before going further, I will take the opportunity to say that I disagree with the notion of self representation. For Freud—and I think he is right—there are only object representations. The ego cannot look at itself. It only has to cope with the representation afforded by the other agencies. One must not confuse the body image with the ego. The ego is no more than a transformation agency relating to reality, accessing motility in order to enhance action. One function plays the role of linking with the subject—identification. After Freud, Lacan has shown that the role of identification is to capture the ego. In the end, I believe that the subject has the right to claim its value as a concept for another reason. The subject is the necessary condition to form a relationship with the Other. This is another concept that we owe to Lacan. It would take too long to have to specify here why the object is not enough. Maybe what is missing in the content of this theory is the emphasis on the paradox that is inherently part of it—that is, being both the same and different, implying that a subject can only communicate with another subject that is, also, precisely the Other. As the Other, it is subjected to disharmonies parallel to those operating in the subject. The subject's recognition of what it is made up of and what it tries to achieve cannot occur unless he is recognized by another subject—the Other—who is marked by corresponding shortcomings but is capable of looking at the subject with the ability to put together some of the fragments—the bits and pieces of its history—that the ego's struggle has failed to integrate. For this, if identification is necessary, it should also be observed that all that is not enough, just as compassion is not enough to cure our patients. What is needed is a recognition of the most unacceptable parts, which are also present in him. The necessity of this concept does not appear in Freud's work, nor in Klein's. A subject can accept all the imperfection of his condition, the awkwardness of his attempts, and his mishappenings if, and only if, he is recognized by another subject. While he had never stated this as I have just done it, Winnicott's work pleads for this interpretation.

The unconscious subject, for Lacan, refers to a set of unconscious operations—condensation, displacement, and many of the other unconscious mechanisms. These have something to do with the structure of internal processes within each person. On the other hand, there is the ego, and that's why I'm talking in this way—because I think that the matrix of this structure is an "ego subject", a *Moi-sujet*. Moreover, the ego's main reference is to the body and the relationship of feelings to the body, and its relationship to reality. It is complemented by the subject, which is the unconscious agent of a set of operations, including the defences. Now we have to come to the object, and the problem of why I included "objects" in the plural in the title. I did that because it is conventional and perhaps mistaken to speak of "object relationship". When we use the singular, it is as if we had thought of one final object, one matrix of the object, which would be responsible for the display of a variety of substructures of the object, and to which we could subsequently turn, keeping the initial model in mind. If you think of psychoanalytic experience, or what happens in one's own life, or the life of others, or the work of—say—Freud, Abraham, Klein, Fairbairn, Winnicott, Lacan, and others, there is no possibility of offering a unifying conception of the object. Not one of these people has succeeded in giving a unifying concept of the object. No matter what theory we refer to, the object can only be defined in relation to some other elements of the theory. Its properties are defined by reference to oppositions, the internal object, the external object, the paternal object, the maternal object, the part object, the whole object, and so on. At the start of this lecture, I gave the example in French of *objectal* and *objectif*, but it is not only in psychoanalysis that it is difficult to have a unifying conception of the object; it is also a task in which philosophy has been engaged, with no more success than psychoanalysis. If you take common experience, the analysis of the object brings out the following points: when you speak of an object, what you infer is the existence of the subject—the subject being affected by the object—and its being responsive to the effects produced by the object.

The first question that this begs is, of course, what there is in the subject that predisposes it to be mobilized, in one way or another, by the object. In banal terms, why do you fall in love with a particular person, whilst some of your close friends may ask themselves what you are attracted to in that person? Secondly, the definition of the object must be related to the topography to which it belongs and to the space in which the object stands. If the subject can be conceived of as the destination of the object, or that which summons the object, then the attributes of the objects are dependent upon the spaces of which they are an integral part. For instance, if we consider (what is called) the "objective object", its attributes are dependent upon the characteristics of the space in which it is located. You can say the same about the internal object. You cannot define the internal object without defining the type of space to which it belongs, and that is why it is so difficult to define. As, for instance, Freud's inner world is clearly presented as the realm of the unconscious: primary processes and afterwards, more deeply, as sheltering instinctual impulses that are seeking discharge. This description does not fit Melanie Klein's inner world, because she does not give any description of the specificity of the processes involved in the description of archaic fantasies, threat of annihilation, etc. Later on, but quite latterly, she will give the description of projective identification. But what about that which is not projected? Persecution and idealization are not just processes, because they can only be understood as contents of an experience, rather than how they induce specific forms of activity. Finally, another problem is the question of the level on which the subject finds itself interested in the attributes of the object, or the way in which the attributes of the object are employed. This can range from affective expressions (which cloud the boundaries between subject and object) to the possibility of knowing the object at a very high level of definition. For all such experiences, we use the same word to define the relationship. One thing is certain, though: the subject is much better equipped for acquiring knowledge about external as opposed to internal objects, probably because the boundaries are not so well defined in the latter.

At least we can come to some provisional conclusions from these remarks. There is always more than one object. I think this is an important statement, because it can bring about the coherence of certain paradigms. Take, for instance, the oedipal structure: this necessarily includes two objects, but it is the result of a development from a two-object to a three-object situation (at least in common thinking about it). The fact that there is always more than one object with the subject means that we have a basic triangular situation. In the beginning, this need not necessarily be the father and mother as distinct people, but may necessitate finding out what the third element is, even in the most apparently dual relationship. For instance, if we think of the "mother–infant relationship", there is a third party: that which is in the mother's mind and is not to do with the baby, but that will also affect the relationship with the baby. The effects of the object on the subject also seem to be impossible to render in a homogenous way. This is not only in the sense that the object is not unique, it is that there is more than one object. The object in itself is not a homogenous structure: its diversity, and the type of material with which the object is linked—body-representation, words, images, thoughts—all this creates a heterogeneous stuff whose diversity challenges the unity of the subject. Finally, I come to a provisional conclusion: it seems that the only way to define the object is to place it in a context where it is defined by its determinants. In reality, it is difficult to find the determinants of the object because there are so many of them. Instead, perhaps we can use a model and transpose our thought onto that. So, let's take the linguistic model, with its syntactical units: subject, verb, object, and so forth. We are not going to take this linguistic matrix and that unity and then apply it to the psychic world, as Lacan did: rather, we are going to try to find its equivalence with psychic reality. Of course, this leads us to consider the difference between ego and subject, between instinct and verb—"objects" remaining the same word in both cases.

Firstly, we will consider the substitution of the ego for the grammatical conception of the subject. As we know, conceptions about the ego have changed a lot. There are very divergent opinions, and psychoanalysts do not agree any more on many points. No one, however, discusses the importance of the unconscious fraction of the ego, and the part played by the instinct in the construction of the object is currently questioned for a great variety of reasons. The role of the object, in the constitution of the ego (through the exchanges between the two), is emphasized, and agreed upon, by almost all authors. But we are still lacking the details of this interaction and the form taken by the outcome. So we now face a difficulty: we have to think in terms of the ego that is subjected to the effects of the object, since that which elaborates any knowledge about the object is itself a weft, woven (at least partially) from its exchanges with the object. Something of the object has passed into the texture of the ego, and we can see this particularly in the mother–child relationship. The structure of the personality of the mother has woven the texture of the ego of the child, but this raises an epistemological problem. How can such a weft be created? The first thing that comes to mind is identification; this seems undeniable. But other more subtle mechanisms have been described. Winnicott, in his paper "Mirror-Role of Mother and Family in Child Development" (1971a), describes a precursor to the mirror stage presented by Lacan. Winnicott assumes that when the infant turns to his mother's face, generally what he sees is himself. A dialectical circle takes place here: the mother looks at the baby, and what her face expresses is in direct relationship with what she sees. However, the expression of the face is not only related to the perception of the baby, but also, as one can expect, the way the mother is affected by what she perceives of her internal mood. It is this complex interaction that is sent forth. In the end, the conclusion is that what the baby gets back, from looking at the mother, cannot be anything else other than himself or what will become of himself. This example can serve to show that the object has come to line the surface of the ego's reception. Along the same lines, I have postulated that the psyche should be conceived of as being structured by two factors: division and complementarity.

There is a tendency to ascribe the "inside" experience to something else perceived externally, as if this has an intimate relationship to what is (confusedly) framed inside. We can see the difference with projection, where what is perceived as coming from outside is, instead, something that has happened inside. In my description, a double identity is settled, which establishes a link between the relationship of oneself to oneself and the relationship of oneself to an Other. This could form the basis of a psychoanalytic concept of metaphor, without one having to think of an established separation between what is felt as "me" and what is felt as the "Other". Because the important thing here is the journey, the "transportation", so to speak, even if the internal and the external spaces have not found definite boundaries yet. Here the main outcome could be the awareness of the Other as similar. It is not enough to say—as it is sometimes written—that the Other gives meaning to the messages sent to him, without having the possibility of clearly knowing what the contents of these messages are. One should say, instead, that it is my own meaning that I perceive in the object because even if I can feel, I can only perceive through the Other. The implication here is that the Other is perceived of as giving clues as to the elaboration of his own internal movement connected with the baby. However, this may remain definitely unconscious.

We can perhaps find some help to explain the most striking effects on the subject provoked by the object, in terms of resonances that are engendered in the ego in response to what the object offers, as a matter for thought and knowledge. However, from what I have said, you can see that the ego responds, because its texture is in resonance with the object of its knowledge. In other words, if the child has to learn something from the mother, it is not only because his ego is dependent on the mother, but also because of the extent to which his ego is woven from the relationship with the mother. Thus, he comes to know something that is already in him, having had it put in him through the exchange with the object. This kind of dialectical relationship can also be seen in the transference. In fact, this is a very theoretical and abstract assessment, which is all based on psychoanalytic experience. What we know from the patient is a response to what we have put into the patient, perhaps in an obscure way that we must decipher. It does not mean that all we know about is what we have put in the patient beforehand, but at least a part of it is, because the relationship there is to what I would call a similar Other and takes form during the process of exchange. We speak of the self and Other, and this is an adequate opposition, but I think that the true opposition is the relationship to the similar Other, *l'autre semblable*; the object is different and distinct, although it is similar. If it were not different, it would not have to be known; and if it was not similar, it could not be known. So, the relationship to the "similar Other" is related to that which responds from within, to the traces left inside from previous experiences, and it is through these exchanges that the "similar Other" can enable its difference to emerge. It is because there is a similarity that there is a possibility of knowledge, but the knowledge leads to awareness of the difference. The interesting thing about the "similar Other" is that while continuing to exist, as for instance in the concept of the neighbour (love thy . . .), this neighbour is also the cause of my hate, precisely because I refuse to recognize aspects of myself in what he is. The echo that I shall be able to experience in the Other as different will arise complementarily. The most achieved accomplishment of this creation is in the oedipal structure, which confronts the subject with the double difference: difference of the sexes and difference of the generations, which links the subject both to his parents and to the Other that he is not.

Let us now turn to the second co-determinant of the object (an equivalent to the verb in the linguistic model)—the instinct in psychoanalysis. There is, of course, a current controversy about the instincts. If you want to be fashionable now, you must not speak of those dirty things called the instincts: they belong to the old-hat Freudian psychoanalysis of the nineteenth century. But when you give some thought to this—the supposed opposition between the instincts on the one hand and object relations on the other—this opposition is very superficial. If you look at Freud's last statements on instincts, you will see that at the end of his life he made some quite important changes, and these changes make the opposition less acute than is usually said. In the *Outline of Psychoanalysis* (1940a [1938]), he opposed the death instinct, and what he had called the life instincts (which he equates with the love instincts). Let's leave the death instinct out of this. If Freud equates life instincts and love instincts, it is obvious that he introduces the concept of the object, because you cannot speak of love unless you include an object. Thus, it was Freud himself who opened the way for the development of what has been called object relations theory, although he had no time to overcome his own contradiction. Furthermore, there is a much more interesting concept in *Beyond the Pleasure Principle* (1920g). In that paper, Freud offered the possibility of an anteriority to the pleasure principle, which was more logical than chronological, and that was the function of binding. Binding, for Freud, is prior to what is considered in terms of relationships, and I think that this paves the way for what has more recently been written regarding object relations. But Freud recognizes that the strongest pleasure coincides with an unbinding of the primary processes. So how can we figure that out? There is an original binding, which comes about through what is called an instinct creating the first form of an organization of material that already belongs to the psyche. As Freud said, this is in a form that is unknown to us, and (I would add) in a form that is unrecognizable by us. This means that, in the deepest layers of our mind—a thing that is very close to bodily structure—there are inclinations or tendencies, and these include the fact that there is some form of continuity or of an elementary, rudimentary organization. It is because there is that form of binding and organization that in a second move the unbinding of the primary processes can release pleasure. It is as if we had to take into consideration the journey through which instinctual activity is relayed by object presentation. To take a very simple example, this means that the cathexis is the interest you take in something, the significance it has for you. So, when there is a pleasure-seeking activity—that is, a tendency towards an object for a certain type of pleasure—then there is the significance and the binding. After the journey from this to the object-presentation (for instance, in the shift from being in quest for pleasure from a specific object), the presentation of the object, from that moment, becomes even more important than the object itself. What happens is that when the object is not there, it is replaced by a framing structure. The presentation of the object is not the figure of the object, nor its shape, nor the image of the object. What I am calling a "framing structure" is very close, I think, to what Winnicott described as "holding". In holding, it is internalization that is important, and that comes about through the absence of the object and the traces that are left behind and internalized. The presentation of the object is also close to what Bion would call a "container".

I have tried to give a more complete view of Freud's model of hallucinatory wish-fulfilment. Thinking of the contemporary models given by Winnicott and Bion, one could propose the following view. In the relationship between mother and infant, Winnicott has factually described the triad as holding, handling, and object presenting. And Bion, at a point where he seems to have overlooked sexuality, unexpectedly proposes a model that combines the masculine and the feminine, and translates them in terms of contained and container. In both cases, it seems important to underline the idea that the space surrounding the baby is of very great importance. Not only is it a space to protect him and to alleviate his anxieties (though this does play a role), but it is also because in some way this could be a first apprehension of his further internal space. When the moment of separation arrives, the qualities will have a fate of their own and will be included in the psychic world, but the mother, as holder or container, undergoes a negative hallucination of herself as a separate body. The qualities calibrated through the pleasure–unpleasure experiences are transformed in the inner world, whereas the holder–container becomes, through this negative hallucination, the framing structure that will form the receptacle for the projection of the internal world, and their working through with further experiences. From this perspective, hallucinatory wish-fulfilment requires the constitution of the screen that is provided through the negative hallucination that forms the framing structure. This framing structure is the obverse of the reverse, formed by the hallucinatory wish-fulfilment.

Another type of binding occurs through language, and what is maintained here is the instinctual cathexis—I mean the interest, the energy, and the force that can detach itself from the imagery, so that the energy is still available and can now invest in new forms of representation, such as words, that also require a great amount of binding. Words have a non-representational equivalence to things. This is the difference between the image, which is supposed to be a kind of copy of the object, and the word, which has no relationship to the appearance of the object. So, it is the importance of cathexis, and the withdrawal of the representation of the object, that can create that secondary binding—the binding of secondary processes. It is also a transformation that occurs because now the instinct is probably replaced by a body ego. Freud defines this as a surface, or that which corresponds to the projection of the surface. I think that this is a very important step, because this bodily ego enables a space for the ego that the ego could perhaps not have had while in the context of instinct and instinct functioning. The relationship to the body (through the different stages from the binding, starting with instinctual activity via object presentation to word and language) has been changed rather than discarded. Through this transformation, the object outside the ego becomes a component part of the structure of the ego, by transmission of the energy into cathexis. This originates in the instinctual sources that propagate in the systems that they cathect, and merges the elements that come from the ego, the object, and the instinct. We have an energy to cathect that is intrinsic to the functioning of the sets thus constituted and able to be converted into different types of presentation—both of the object and from the functioning in which it participates. What I am trying to grasp here is the functioning of the mind and the system of transformation from the early dependence of the child to its body and its mother's body, to autonomy and to the functioning of thought (part of which is some distance from the object and the instincts). The traces of the presentation in the mind are always in flux, because a relationship to the instincts is always dynamic.

It is rather a long way into this lecture, but now we come to psychoanalytic experience and the transference phenomena. What is striking in the psychoanalytic experience is that we all have the feeling that the analyst is a unique type of object that has no equivalent in the ordinary conditions of human relationships. What is interesting is that in discussions of this we deliberately fail to define any of the characteristics that belong to the analyst as an object, but on the other hand we are eager to talk about the attributes of the setting. We define the attributes of the space, of the type of relationship—the psychoanalytic contract—but we do not define the characteristics of the object that is in that space. Of course, what we believe is that the setting will define for the patient the attributes and the characteristics of the object—what we usually call projections. I propose, instead, that the best way to define the setting is as a system that can function without directly intervening in the analytic process. The setting is a kind of catalytic or inductive function, which does not take part in the process, but without which the process cannot take place. If you think of it, this is exactly what Freud says when, in his paper "Formulation on the Two Principles of Mental Functioning" (1911b), he speaks of the closed system at the beginning. It is a system that is submitted to the pleasure and unpleasure principles. He recognizes the impossibility of maintaining such an organization that can only exist thanks to the care it receives from the mother. Winnicott took that up and gave it its full importance. Freud thought that the system could function as long as one includes maternal care; even though maternal care was outside the system, it was something that allowed the system to function, without intervening directly in the exchanges of the system that are regulated by the pleasure and unpleasure principles. This is a very important concept, particularly in the light of Winnicott's idea of potential space that takes place in the process of reunion after separation. Could it be possible that this accomplishment has to rely on this previous catalytic relationship? Of course, you also have to think of all the systems that are catalytic or inductive and that do not directly intervene in the relationship between you and your patient. They are indispensable for the relationship to function—such as, for instance, free-floating attention, or neutrality. In themselves, they do not influence the situation, but they are absolutely necessary for the development of the relationship. The analytic relationship will lead to the awareness of the experience of the non-ego. The important thing is to be aware that there are two kinds of non-ego. Using Winnicott's terms, we can speak of the conscious not-me and the unconscious not-me. We experience the latter when a patient responds to an interpretation with, "Oh that's not what I meant, well, I didn't want to mean that. I cannot recognize myself in what you say." The conscious not-me will be the other—the object—which is outside the subject and distant from it. So the whole interplay will be between these two parts of the not-me. The crux of the matter is the way in which a relationship will be established with that outside ego, and also with the unconscious non-ego—the two parts of the not-me.

To some extent, the sign of an analysis that is progressing is the self-appropriation of the not-me—the unconscious becoming conscious. The question then arises about what happens to the object and whether there is a possibility of self-appropriation of the non-ego—that is, outside the subjective experience. What happens here, I think, is an awareness that the object, the not-me that is outside me and is not unconscious, cannot be appropriated. Some things can be appropriated from it, which we call incorporation, or introjection, or internalization; but the Other will always remain the Other. I will never be able to make the real Other a property of mine, and this is something that comes into play at the end of some analyses. In speaking of appropriation, one is speaking of links, and it is of course within the general framework of psychoanalytic experience that one of the guidelines of the experience is how the ego extracts itself from its relationship with the internal object and relates to an object outside himself. The distinction between ego and object will be facilitated by the cohesion of his ego and how he manages to save this cohesion while establishing a relationship with an object that requires a loosening of this coherence, to make himself open to the influence and demands of an object that is different from him. This is what the analytic situation can test, when the ego is confronted with experiences that it has to take in, and that finds its sources in parts of the mind that are out of its control. Like Winnicott, I believe that observation falls short, because I think that the hypotheses of Freud are imaginative constructions, because of the difficulty of thinking about the action of an instinct, coupled with the necessity of producing a substratum of unobservable phenomena of the mind.

The instincts can be conceived of as forces inspiring trends and internal movements that have to be integrated in sets of manageable exchanges. A great deal of the transformational processes that take place are not available to memory. Therefore, psychoanalysis is based not only on empathy, but also on deduction. Freud said that the transference was never obvious; it is not observable, and has to be deduced instead. I'm afraid that in giving so much importance to observation, one remains in the field of the observable, whereas, to me, the peculiarity of the mind really is that it deals with unobservable phenomena. To bring back observation is to return to the idea that the mind could be reachable through the senses, because either the mind of the observer goes beyond the senses and he has to explain how his inferences are constructed, or it is dependent on the senses and what it deals with is everything except the mind. Here I align myself with Bion, who said that psychoanalysis relies on an experience that is not a sensuous experience. According to Freud—I do not want to read quotations—the object is born out of experience but is mainly a construction of the mind. We try to grasp its function through the way it appears in the analysis, or in the analyst who has to analyse. It is not by chance that analysis deliberately deprives itself of the resources of the senses, except the senses linked to language. The way the ego has to perform its tasks when it has to deal with the object is quite different from when it has to deal with the drives.

We can describe a certain type of relationship of the ego in terms of appropriation of the object it relates to. The part of the ego that has assimilated the object is known to us through identification. This is the part of the ego that is originally considered as belonging to object attributes. It refers to the objects as a possession of the ego. It is also connected to the part of the ego that is moved through desire. Desire is the movement that brings about the awareness of the relationship of the ego to what is not he, but is also not outside the ego. It is that part of him, the part that is transformable, in the prospect of enrichment through the realization of satisfactions, old and new ones. This opens up the field for sublimation, an aspect that is, to me, irreducible to a full appropriation, and finally an aspect that serves as a support for the creation of new objects.

Now, another way of appraising other aspects of the ego is the function in relation to the instincts. Here, I shall mention a series of the object's functions, which I will just quote. I think that the appraisal of the object is dependent on a cathexis function: the object is proposed as a receptacle for cathexes and becomes the object of a space where the cathexes give it the potential power to recognize other cathexes, and even to transfer itself to them. There is a function of the object—that is, the function of reflection—which is produced by the cathected object and, after transformation, is sent back to its origin and source. There is a framing function, about which I have already said a little. There is a perceptibility function, which is to do with the presence and the absence of the object and what happens in these circumstances. There is an acceptability function: acceptability is the ability of the ego to find itself returning to give and to receive pleasure, in spite of the fact that the awareness of the independence of the object has generated hate. There is an illusion function, which I do not need to explain. There is also an attraction function, a satisfaction function, a substitution function, a function regulating the conditions that provoke anxiety, an induction function, and finally a creation function.

I am sorry to just enumerate these functions, which I have developed elsewhere (Green, 1995). From all of these functions, we can see the polymorphous functionality of the object and the way it establishes its relationship with the ego and the subject. The primary link to the object is the instinctual attachment to the body of the mother. The body of the child is attached to another object as well as to that object's body. The child is attached to the mother, who herself is attached to someone else—the Other of the object. It is necessary to clarify the thinking about the mother–child relationship, which has been a little bit over-simplified. The mother–child relationship—which is so often the backdrop for the object relationship—could be described in such a way as to consider first a co-present pole. It is co-present with the child—the mother has an amorous feeling towards the child, which is shown actively by making use of an aim-inhibited instinct and passively by accepting to serve as the object in order to satisfy the aim-uninhibited instinct of the child. Uninhibited instincts belong to the other co-present pole—this is the child of the earliest phases, watched over by the mother's own repression. In very simple terms, it means that the mother offers herself to be the satisfaction of the child's uninhibited instincts, and she responds to the child by aim-inhibited instincts. She also offers herself to the father and shares with him the pleasure of aim-uninhibited instincts (as far as repression allows). The specific nature of the mother is that she is the only element of the triangle (constituted by child, mother, and father) to have a bodily instinctual relationship with the two others. The two others have only one relationship to her; the child and the father having no bodily relationship with each other of an immediate nature. (I refuse, by the way, to accept the argument that "new fathers" also take care of their babies: they are—even if they manage quite well—intrinsically incompetent, and they have no idea what a pregnancy is, as the mother knows, smiling with indulgence.)

Another co-present pole is the child, who alternately experiences an uninhibited instinct that authorizes an instinctual discharge, during which the accompanying satisfaction drains the part object. The child has a double type of functioning: one type with the possibility of discharging the aim-uninhibited instinct (for instance, when he feeds from and gets the breast), and another type, which will take place as aim-inhibited instincts are on the verge of opening a dialogue with the object. Winnicott has shown very explicitly that the consummation and the discharge obtained by pleasure consumes the object, and it will disappear as a result. The role of these other aim-inhibited instincts—those that are related, for instance, to tenderness rather than sensuality—is to enable the child not to make the mother disappear through the discharge of pleasure. And, finally, a third pole, which is co-present for the mother and absent for the child, is the father. This is why we say that, in the beginning, the father does not exist for the child. He still, of course, exists for the mother: he is in her mind, and he shares the enjoyment of sexuality with her, and he also takes part in the development of motherhood. The mother may have many objects inside herself, of course—her father, grandfather, mother, sister—but for the child there is only one distinct object that will come into effective existence as a thought-pole in its own right—the father. The function of the father—this is what Lacan emphasized—is that he is the agent who separates the child from the body of the mother. The problem is: to whom does the mother's body belong?—to no one exclusively, and not even to herself.

To conclude, I will now move back to the functions that I was discussing earlier, and I will end by defending the existence of an objectalizing function. What I mean by this is that psychic activity acquires the ability to transform not only objects, but also any activity or function of the mind, into an object. Any type of existence that is significant to the child can be transformed into an internal object. Winnicott showed us the existence of the transitional object. This really is the evidence that anything can be transformed into an object, since it can be anything elected by the baby for that use. There are other examples to show that this can happen in the mind—that the ego can transform reality to make it a part of itself and then be nourished by these internal objects. For instance, a very common example is sublimation. If, say, a person paints, not only do the paintings become objects, but also the very activity of painting itself (which can remain even in the absence of any painting) becomes an object to which he can give his life if he is an artist.

One wonders whether the aim of the objectalizing function (which transforms the cathexes linked to the object in such a way that they themselves become objects) is not an enterprise designed to provide internal possession for the ego. Thus, the ego will not be left with its narcissism running on the spot because of the limits that are imposed on instinctual satisfaction. In this way, the limitations of failure to encounter the search for satisfaction are able, by giving object-like traits to cathexes, to bring the form of objectalization to them as a memory, so that the ego can recognize itself in a constantly renewable actualization. To some extent, this is a way to comfort the subject about the permanence of the primitive objects, even though those primary parental objects are now replaced by these very sophisticated objects. Perhaps, through the passage of time, we become the parents of the internal objects that we have created in ourselves.

THREE

On thirdness

It is remarkable that Freud, who invented psychoanalysis, the analysis of the psyche, never gave any definition of the psychical. Each time he had to make a statement about it he said there was no point because everyone knew intuitively or by experience what he meant. However much his statement was justified from the point of view of common sense, it is not a very scientific one. We would not expect a physicist to deal with concepts such as matter or energy in a similar way. In the general subject index of the *Standard Edition*, "psychical" occupies an entire page of two columns, but it was not until 1938 that Freud mentioned the problem of the nature of the psychic, in an unfinished paper whose original title was "Some Elementary Lessons in Psycho-Analysis" (1940b [1938]), which is a sort of *Outline* written in English in London shortly before his death. I quote:

> If someone asks what "the psychical" really means, it is easy to reply by enumerating its constituents: our perceptions,

---

This *Squiggle* Public Lecture was given on 25 May 1991 at Primrose Hill Community Centre, London.

ideas, memories, feelings and acts of volition—all these form part of what is psychical. But if the questioner goes further and asks whether there's not some common quality possessed by all these processes which make it possible to get nearer to the nature or, as people say, the essence of the psychical, then, it is harder to give an answer. [p. 282]

We know that Freud fought against the general opinion of equating the psychic with the conscious. He objected, saying that what is conscious cannot be the essence of what is psychic, consciousness being only a quality (among other possibilities) of the psychic. On the contrary, he defined the idea that the psychic, whatever its nature may be, was in itself unconscious. Unfortunately, Freud did not fully develop his views beyond what he had already said on the topic: the manuscript ends before he is able to give the answer as to the nature of the psychic. He needed to insist that being conscious could not be the "essence", the most intimate feature, by which it can be grasped by the mind. Today we take it for granted that Freud's observation about the existence of unconscious phenomena belongs to the psyche, but we should also remind ourselves about some other statements by Freud in the same 1938 paper—for instance, that psychology is a natural science. We can see now that our present way of thinking about science does not always fit in with Freud's statement. It is not only a question of refusing with him to define the psychic only by reference to consciousness and to postulate the existence of the unconscious, it is also that our ideas about some current views are not very clear—for instance, about the opposition between psychology and biology. "Psychology too is a natural science", says Freud, "What else can it be?" As Winnicott observed later, the science that should help to explain the disorders of emotional development or the distortions of personality and character—the science that corresponds to anatomy and physiology in physic medicine—has not yet attained firm roots. "One may ask, in fact, whether this science has yet been named because certainly the name psychology does not meet the situation" (R. Gaddini, personal communication). So it is here not so much a question of opposition but, rather, an attempt to delineate something specific that is very difficult to define. One could say that Winnicott's work is entirely devoted to trying to advance the problem.

Let us come back to Freud. He writes that psychoanalysis is a part of the mental science of psychology. So, if psychoanalysis is part of the mental science of psychology (itself being a part of the natural science), the question I raise is, "What psychology do we need to understand the nature of the psychic?" Currently it is agreed that one of the significant attainments of American psychoanalysis, through the ideas of Hartmann, is to have added to Freud's three points of view of metapsychology—the dynamic, the topographic, and the economic—two others: the genetic and the structural. These statements are not accepted everywhere (especially beyond the borders of the United States), and many European analysts consider these additions as debatable. The adaptive perspective raises enormous criticism, accusing psychoanalysts of acting as representatives of social conformism and willing to adjust the patient to society. *This is not the analyst's task and indeed goes against his values.* Respect for the patient's freedom of choice is an inescapable aim of psychoanalysis. As for the genetic point of view, things are subtler and more complicated. At a certain period in the history of psychoanalysis, under the influence of some important figures, it was hoped that infant observation would provide the theory of psychoanalysis with safe ground in order to counteract excessive speculation. Melanie Klein's ideas were discussed, and most of them were rejected by the majority of psychoanalysts. Observation would show how improbable they were. That did not stop Melanie Klein's ideas spreading all over the world, and what happened then was that the Kleinians too started to observe infants and to conclude that their observations confirmed Melanie Klein's ideas (see the work of Esther Bick). However, it is evident that the same child, when seen through the eyes of Spitz, Mahler, Winnicott, or Stern, induced very different observations, conclusions, theoretical statements, etc. It is impossible to deny that mere facts hardly exist in this field, and that the simplest statements depend on the observers' references, not to say beliefs. To take one example: how many years of scientific observations passed before an eccentric gentleman described what he called a "transitional object" (Winnicott, 1951)? This was something that had been known by any mother for millennia. Most of the time, the evidence was in the eyes of the observer, not in the child's behaviour. Freud's science was considered as insufficiently scientific.

Metapsychology was declared wrong and useless. For a time, it was thought that psychoanalysis could gain a lot of knowledge in exploring fields that lent themselves to investigations, such as the effects of extraordinary circumstances on the child's emotional development. The Second World War provided such opportunities, and soon other situations allowed important findings, such as in the field of hospitalization. In an extension of these new attitudes towards the unknown features of psychic activity there came about a shift of emphasis from what had been investigated up to then and used to belong to the consequences of the repression of forbidden wishes or drives, to the influence of external traumas. This also led to trying to observe the significant events from the outside and to link them to the consequences that seemed to have a direct relationship. Obviously, what was minimized was the still very mysterious internal work that took place between the two. What happened in fact—and was not always noticed—was that the more we seemed to throw light on the supposed ego mechanisms (to which new attention was paid), the more we lost sight of the ways in which they related to the unconscious and even more—needless to say—to its radical roots, specified by Freud as the id. This work was intrinsically internal. Even external factors, like traumas, could not be considered without the reaction (which included the drives in that exceptional unbalance), as if external events could be interpreted by the young psyche as originating in the internal world. What remained obscure, defeating our efforts to arrive at some sort of transparency, which is one of the characteristics of the unconscious was—at length—unacceptable.

At the beginning of these researches, it was agreed that academic psychology did not help to explain the facts dealt with by psychoanalysis. But little by little what in fact happened was that the new psychology—ego-psychology and its development—looked more and more like the one that it was proposed to replace. And as a consequence the discrepancy between the core of psychoanalysis (as Freud's work had developed) and the relationship between the new fashionable "ego" and the realm of what Freud called the instincts (which you may call today by any other term, if you wish, as long as you still keep in mind what it is about) became less and less understandable: for example, Hartmann's idea of a conflict-free sphere—of an ego with no relationship to the id—

or, later, Kohut's idea of a self that is also independent from the drives. These sorts of ideas became a new focus for both theory and therapy, and yet were extremely far from the basic hypotheses of Freudian analysis. We all know that the psychology of the psyche cannot be the psychology of the ego, because the psychology of the ego was what existed before psychoanalysis was created. We still have to consider very seriously the literal meaning of metapsychology. If Freud's intention was to give up metaphysics and to replace it by metapsychology, this last body of conceptions could not be reduced to psychology. What was beyond psychology—metapsychology—was also what was beyond consciousness. No psychology could be applied to what is unconscious, as Winnicott intuitively understood.

The psyche, Freud says, is a function of an apparatus. It is interesting to note that for Freud the basis of psychic function is the drives, and that he has always stood against any drive monism. He disagreed with the conception of one basic drive that subdivided into many others, and he preferred a dualistic conception throughout his life. He even defined the functioning of partial drives in terms of pairs of opposites. It is not only in connection with the drives that we find dualistic oppositions, we can also think of the two series of *processes*, primary and secondary; two types of *repression*, primary and secondary; and also of fantasies, primary and secondary, etc. Most of Freud's notions or concepts are divided into two classes opposing each other. There are two notable exceptions: the psychic apparatus and the Oedipus complex. It is noticeable that as far as basic mechanisms or processes are concerned, Freud chooses to present them in a dualistic view, but when he refers to complex structures, thirdness is necessary. A current opinion considers (according to the genetic viewpoint) that two precedes three in numbers. From a developmental perspective, the dual relationship—or in other words, the mother–infant relationship—is at the beginning the "pre-oedipal relationship" and precedes the oedipal stage, which involves three persons. So, from a developmental perspective it would be logical to shift these relationships from a two-part to a three-part one. Winnicott rightly said that "there is no such thing as a baby", meaning that one has always to consider the baby in relation to something else—his mother, the environment, the cradle, or whatever. I would like to add to this that there is no such thing as a mother–infant relationship. I say that, of course, as a reminder of the role of the father, otherwise it is too simplistic a view. While it is obvious that a baby in the very beginning is related exclusively to the maternal object, this is no reason for considering that the father has no existence whatsoever during that period. It is also obvious, at least to me, that the quality of a good-enough relationship on the part of the mother will depend on the mother's love for the father and vice-versa, even if the child's relationship to the father seems minimal, compared to the bond with the mother in the earliest time of life. The matter at issue, and that is of the utmost importance, is whether in a relationship the actual partners of a situation are those who are effectively present or whether an absent party can play a role by virtue of being present in the mind of one of the members of the couple. Here Winnicott's ideas can be usefully completed with some of Bion's. Considering the primary modes of organization in the development of the infant, Bion quickly arrives at the conclusion that explanations in terms of the good and bad breast are inadequate, as if he implied that in order to build the psychic, something else (that also belongs to the psyche and is indispensable to its creation) is needed. And this is how he postulates the existence of the alpha function, which he originates in the mother's "capacity for reverie". What is involved here is that even if the mother feeds the child adequately, this alone will not do in order to favour, to promote (to create?) thinking. The mother herself has to think—in some special way—in order to help the child to overcome his tendency to reject what he feels as painful, a result that will always prove ineffectual because of the tendency of what has been rejected to re-invade its birthplace. When Bion comes to describe the process in detail, he tells us what the mother's reverie is about. He emphasizes that if the reverie is not tuned by a love for the baby, nor for the father, this fact will be transmitted to the infant, even if it is a fact felt as incomprehensible. Here is a convincing example of what I am trying to say about the role of a third party, not directly present in the relationship but nevertheless conveyed, in absentia, through a member of the couple of the actual relationship. *It should be emphasized that Bion's model was not drawn from any observation setting, but rather from his deductions borne out of his experience in the analytic setting with psychotic patients.*

I do not think that one has to wait until the child is capable of conceiving of that third person (through language, for instance) before admitting that it can be influenced by the presence in the mother's mind of her fantasies about the father. I propose to name this the "other of the object" (that which is not the subject). The third element is not restricted to the person of the father; it is also symbolic. In the mother's mind, the third element reduplicates alongside the real person of the father. What Lacan has named the paternal metaphor emphasizes that the concept of fatherhood links the father as the absent element in the mother's mind with other significant figures of her past—for instance, the traces that stand for her own father or mother, which represent her childhood fantasies that are connected with the wish of receiving a child from a parental figure, even beyond her parents. In certain cases, a real closed dual relationship can occur, but here I am alluding to relationships from which the father or the third figure is radically excluded, or, even more, annihilated, foreclosed from the mother's desire, as Lacan said. This is a fateful precondition for mental illness and paves the way for subsequent psychosis or, if not, for other major psychic disorders. To discuss the situation properly we need to use another description that will account for important distinctions.

The three partners—the child, the mother, and the father—have different statuses according to their being present or absent towards each other. The infant is co-present with the mother and mainly related to her body. He moves from fusion and dependence to separation and independence. Fusion is at the beginning; in spite of some clues showing the possibility of innate isolated reactions, alternate states of fusion and separation follow the first stage. Separation is achieved as the acquisition of the sense of independence grows. (Because of the limitations of time and space, we have to postpone a detailed description of how this can be achieved.) On the other hand, the father is absent for the child. The mother is co-present with the child, of course, but one has to be reminded that the mother is the only partner of the triangle to have a bodily relationship both to the baby and to the father as well. This situation generates conflict to a higher degree for her, because of mixing up tenderness and sensuality and having to untangle them as well. So if she is co-present with the child in an intimate closeness, while thinking of the father, she is absent from the child to a certain degree whilst still being with him. She can cope with the situation by articulating an indirect bond between child and father through her own desires.

The father is co-present with the mother and absent for the child, and, although he may have a bodily relationship with the child, he is not a distinct object at the beginning, nor can his bodily relationship with the child be compared, by any means, with that of the mother. If his presence for the mother is not constant, he can only fully and totally enjoy pleasure from the mother's body by sharing the joy of sexuality with her. How can the traces of the sexual relationship with the father be totally dissociated and split off from the mother's feelings about her own body when she is with the child? This calls for an important repression. She will also have to match the traces of the awakening of her sensuality while she had been with the father with the undeniable sensuous impressions stemming from her relationship with her child. If she is careful to repress in her mind a too direct linkage between both situations, it will be the child who, by his own stimulations, will enhance a forced return of the repressed. It is striking to read all the literature about the mother–infant relationship as if sexuality were totally absent from the picture.

The real problem with the developmental perspective is not the journey from two to three—from the dyad to the triad—but the transition from the stage of potential thirdness (when the father is only in the mother's mind) to effective thirdness when he is perceived as a distinct object by the child. In other words, this is the journey from father residing internally in the mother's mind to the stage when he becomes present in the child's perception of his existence as well as his representation. Needless to say, I am alluding here to a situation long before the so-called oedipal phase. The important thing to emphasize is the meeting of two supposedly independent sequences: the first is the separation between mother and child on the way towards independence, and the second is the association of the awareness of the third party as an obstacle between the partners of the previous relationship. Instead of considering these two series independently, or even describing their succession in time, I propose to look at the situation from the point of view of the unconscious: the two operations are so tightly linked that they are connected logically. From the moment that the mother seems to have escaped from the child's control—which is also another way of stating the child's renunciation of the omnipotence over the object—it is as if she had fallen under the power of the third partner, who gets hold of what has been given up, mostly against his will, by the child. It is not only a matter of how many people are involved in a relationship where thirdness comes into play. We can think of the analytic situation now with a similar perspective.

Analysis was labelled in the 1950s as a "two-body psychology". This new approach was used to emphasize that the analyst's part was underestimated in the psychoanalytic process. Freud has admitted, very late, in "Constructions in Analysis" (1937d), that analysis consisted of two quite different places "involving two people to each of whom a distinct task is assigned" (p. 258). Further reflection by people like Winnicott and Bleger made us aware of a third factor. It was not only a consideration that dealt with the condition of possibilities in practising analysis, but also the setting itself was seen as having to do with attributes of the psychic world that could be seen from a new angle. As if the expression of the inner world could be transposed into the limited field of interaction between subject and object and could reflect characteristics other than those usually deduced from a relationship between two parties standing in the external world. As if something poured from the internal to the external and would give birth to another form of existence before it would become entirely defined by its exteriority. A transitional state between symbiosis (Bleger) and potential reunion (Winnicott), which would reflect partially a hallmark of the location from which it was born, through inhabiting a different space. In Winnicott's view, this was connected with symbolization, seen here not only as the instant reunion of parts that had been separated beforehand, but also including a historical dimension that linked two moments. The reunion was conceived of as a realization of an instant that was only potentially anticipated long before it happened, but when it happened it could not acquire its meaning without being connected with the moment when the parts were split. It is obvious that Winnicott's hypothesis cannot be dissociated from Freud's basic assumption on desire. In symbolization two parts of a broken unity are reunited and the total result can be considered not only as the rebuilding of a lost unity, but also as a third element that is distinct from the two other split-off parts. This way of understanding symbolization obviously links it with conception. To conceive is here to form a concept as well as to imagine a gap between the two states of separation and reunification. Binding and unbinding are the two main functions that Freud found to be the basic characteristics of life or love instincts on the one hand and of destructive instincts on the other hand. This comes close to what I was just stating in terms of reunion and separation. Two functions seem quite enough to explain the interplay of these basic activities, but I wish to propose a third element: rebinding, which corresponds to reunion after separation. Most of the time psychic structures appear to us as already bound. In fact they are less bound than rebound, stemming from an unknown stage where the constituting parts were separated. You tell a dream, you associate, and you analyse it. You break the manifest dream as a bound unity. You disassemble the former apparent unity through the associations. Afterwards a new unity appears in the mind after the dream work has been mobilized again and interpreted. The elements coming under the scrutiny of analysis are rebound into a new unity.

In 1972, I proposed to add to Freud's description of primary and secondary processes another type of mental event—which I call the tertiary processes ("Note sur les processus tertiaires", 1972). Their role is crucial in the course of analysis. The tertiary processes are processes that function as a go-between and link primary and secondary processes. In analytic work they go back and forth, from fantasy to a set of ideas, or from a rational association to the remembering of a dream, not to say from a narrative to an inadvertent slip. The silent work of such processes is what enables the analytic process to progress towards insight. It is also the lack of such processes, or their impairment, which Bion has described in his paper "Attacks on Linking" (Bion, 1962), that accounts for the absence of progress of the analysis. A similar view could also apply to Winnicott's idea of the inability to play or the lack of a transitional area in some patients (Winnicott, 1951).

My next point is a more theoretical one. Having considered the triangular relationship—of child, mother, father—the three basic mechanisms—binding, unbinding, rebinding—and the three categories of primary, secondary, and tertiary processes, I will now turn to what I consider a main feature of the psychic: its relationship to language and thought. Saussure's linguistics were used by Lacan to illustrate his theory according to which the unconscious is structured like a language. Lacan's theory of psychoanalysis was supposed to pay attention only to the signifier and not, by any means, either to the signified or to the meaning related directly to it. The structuralistic reinterpretation, around the 1960s, defended the view that the aim of the cure was to analyse the relationship of the subject to the signifier. In Saussure's linguistic conception, the signifier is the acoustic or material face of the sign. Lacan gave his own definition, which differed a great deal from Saussure's. It was the following: "The signifier is what represents a subject for another signifier" (Lacan, 1955–56). The meaning of this statement may seem obscure. We have to understand that Lacan is speaking here of the signifiers of the unconscious, which form a chain. Therefore, if one considers the relationship between two of them, their connection is understandable only if the operation of a subject is inferred to link them together. Such a subject is, of course, the subject of the unconscious. The signifier, which in language is the smallest unity of language, is represented by its material stuff through which it is signifying by taking part in a system of combination and taken as a model. Applied to psychoanalysis, the isolation of a signifier in a chain induces the operation of the subject, which is detected by the transition from one signifier to the other. At any rate, here you can see the circularity of Lacan's definition—psychoanalysis is the relationship of the subject to the signifier as that which represents the subject for another signifier. To state it in another way—it is the relationship from the subject of the unconscious to the subject of discourse and in his own idiom, his expressions, words, style, etc., which pave the road to unconscious desire, from the most explicit meaningful sentences to the inadvertent turn of phrase. This position can be clarified by another Lacanian axiom: the unconscious receives from the Other his message in an inverted form. This is a generalization of the model of language applied to the unconscious as a discourse of the Other. I shall remark once more that the definition of signifier by Lacan includes a reference to the representation: "what represents a subject for another signifier" (Lacan, 1955–56). In my view, this reference to representation in Lacan's words has the value of a slip of the tongue because he wanted to avoid a conception of the subject in terms of representations as understood in psychoanalytic theory. In spite of the difference in meaning of both uses of representation, the more abstract use of the definition of the signifier could not help coming back to it. Lacan is then bound to do what he tries to escape. Inadvertently we have to match his conception with the Freudian theory of representation. The Lacanian definition of the signifier is quite compatible with Freud's formulation of secondary processes: relationships of relationships.

For me, the concept of representation is, without a shadow of a doubt, the cornerstone of Freud's conception of the psychic apparatus, so long as one does justice to the originality and complexity of the different types of representation included by Freud's conceptual system. Lacan's theory of the signifier restricts the psychoanalytic conception of representation to the representation of a linguistic structure, leaving us in great obscurity as to what represents the subject in the process of a non-linguistic structure. Anyhow, even when he seemed to have advocated an analogy, he tried to conceptualize a system in which the concept of signifier was kept out of the structure from which it acquired its meaning and function. This involved Lacan being compelled to propose a view of the unconscious described in its own right, and he had to enlighten the application of a concept that was drawn from the linguistic field and was admitted to be irrelevant about the material to which it was supposed to apply.

At close scrutiny, Lacan's formulation of the definition of the signifier is indebted to other similar statements borrowed from the great American philosopher and semiotician Charles Sanders Peirce. Peirce did not take into consideration Saussure's distinction between the signifier and the signified, because his interest is in signs beyond the linguistic field. Peirce's semiotic theory is a very complex one, and I do not want to give the impression that I share all of his ideas, because I am not sure of understanding all of them. One of the most striking findings of Peirce is his triadic conception of the sign: firstness, secondness, thirdness. Firstness is associated with qualities of feelings and emotion, secondness with being, and thirdness with generalization such as law, thought processes, and so on. What Peirce has called the "logic of relatives" varies sometimes in the definition of its constituents. Firstness will be characterized in some writing as referring to presence, simplicity, spontaneity, or also as a mode of being in itself. More explicitly, its quality is that of sensations or feelings. Qualifying it as primal or primitive, he emphasizes that his category has no relationship whatsoever with any possibility of anything else other than itself. Secondness, which is in his view the easiest category to grasp, is the result, in its mode of being, of the brutal reaction of a force originating from outside. Here Peirce combines the idea of separateness and reunion in two, and only two, subjects—a principle of constant duality and, as such, not fully comprehensible because the elements, which are either separated or united, form couples, as if nothing else would nor could exist. It is secondary to firstness but does not substitute it. Finally, thirdness is the true level of understanding because it is about the modification of the being of a subject, which cannot modify a pair in any way without introducing something different in nature from the unity of the pair.

These ideas, which were expressed for the first time in 1867 and endlessly enriched up to the end of Peirce's work, ring a bell to the psychoanalyst: firstness is linked with sensations and affects and secondness with conflict and to some extent with primary processes; finally, thirdness applies not only to secondary processes but to what Lacan has defined as the symbolic and Bion as alpha function. Winnicott has cautiously stood between primary creativity and objective perception. As he said, this paradox should not be overcome—that is, we have to accept that objective perception does not supersede primary creativity. The result of their interaction is the enrichment of creativity through objective perception, rather than the substitution of its type of activity dominating the form of thinking about primary creativity.

Peirce's assignment of firstness associated with feelings and secondness with being is in concordance with Freud's paper "Negation" (1925h). Peirce postulates the first type of functioning of the psychic apparatus as based on the judgement of attribution which decides that something is good or bad. Then comes in, secondly, the judgement of existence, which has to decide whether or not the thing exists, in reality. We find here implicitly a common concern: that of placing existence—that is, reality—in the second instance and not in the first one. Let us come to thirdness: here it is associated with the treatment of symbols. All specifically "mental" characteristics of what mental implies are thirdness. Peirce says, in a letter to Lady Wellby, "Thirdness is the triadic relation existing between a sign, its object and the interpreting thought, itself a sign, a sign that mediates between the interpreter and its origin (Peirce, 1931, Vol. III, Book 2, Letter 12).

I do not expect you to find this definition self-evident on a first reading. The relationship between a sign and its object is not enough to understand the way signs function. One has to take the interpreting thought into account. This interpreting thought is itself a sign of a different type—the thought as a sign that is included in a set of signs. Say we are speaking of qualities attributed to an object when we link them to an interpretative thought—what we are dealing with is that part of the object that can be subjected to what can be said about it, or how we or others are related to it, therefore activating the interpreting thought. This, within the evaluating structure, can be found as the sign of the subjective position. It reminds me of Freud's beginnings, even before the birth of psychoanalysis in 1891, around his investigation of aphasia, where he is in search of some basic principles of explanation. He comes to define the symbol as a relationship not between a thing and a word, but between the representation of the thing and the representation of the word.

This type of sign, which is involved in thinking, constitutes the mode of being of a sign, and this will perhaps become clearer as I progress in my exposition. Every analyst is aware of the importance of Freud's findings from the analysis of the Wolf Man (1918b), not only because of the discovery of the primal scene but also because for the first time in psychoanalysis there is a first apprehension of borderline thinking. It is probably the neglect of this aspect of the patient that has been the cause of the most famous reported failure of the analytic treatment. At the end of his paper (after mentioning the far-reaching instinctive [in German *instinktiv*] knowledge of animals), Freud writes: "If human beings too possessed an instinctive endowment such as this . . ." (p. 120); he then goes on to describe the relationship between this type of primitive knowledge and more developed intellectual thinking, which supersedes the previous, though not suppressing it entirely. In particular circumstances the instinctive knowledge may be endowed with a renewed power. "It would not be surprising that it should be very particularly concerned with the processes of sexual life, even though it could not be by any means confined to them. This instinctive factor would then be the nucleus of the unconscious, a primitive kind of mental activity which would later be dethroned and overlaid by human reason, when the faculty came to be acquired, but which in some people, perhaps in everyone, would retain the power of drawing down to it the higher mental process" (Freud, 1918b, p. 120). This quotation supports the idea that as far as instincts are concerned, Freud's conception is obviously not of a biological nature but, rather, alludes to a primitive kind of mental activity. Something that is at the heart of the nature of the psychic—this primitive kind of mental functioning—must have some relationship with what he called the "psychical representative of the drive or the instinct". I want now to spell out what I am alluding to in Freud's quote. The psychic representative of the drive, in his own term, is the *psychische Repräsentanz*: it must not be confused with what is called in English the "ideational representative" [*Vorstellungsrepräsentanz*]. What is the point about this distinction? The difference lies for me in what is represented in each case. The ideational representative refers to the object presentation—i.e. the representation of the idea of the object, in other words, its contents. For instance, if we think of the breast, what is referred to is the attempt to make the breast reappear, even more than the idea of the breast. Whatever it is, it is what we can figure out as being derived by the sense impression of the breast which is in our mind, with the wish to make it come to life again. The psychic representative is the representation of the body stimuli in need of satisfaction that is supposed to reach the mind. This is quite different from the representation of the breast in terms of its ideational content, whether an image or simply an evocation of any of its qualities that are present in its memory traces. In this last instance the image in the mind has a reference outside the mind, in the external world. Does the image look like that which it refers to, and what are the consequences of the conformity or nonconformity of bringing together the image and its outside model? These questions were major problems that Freud met with in his early findings. On the other hand, when we speak of the psychic representative of the drive, there is no external reference. This is not a copy of an original existing anywhere that we can visualize or perceive in our mind, nor to which we can refer as a form. It would be like a movement without image seeking an object to find satisfaction and, if not, turning at least to the traces of a former experience that brought satisfaction. But what is represented here is the move in search of something.

In other words, the instinct or the drive is stated as *being* the representative of the body, and elsewhere the drive as seen by Freud is also stated as *having* representatives (ideational, imaginary, affective, verbal, and so on) to which it will turn when reality does not bring the satisfaction. So, the instinct connects the being with the demands of the body. But that being is dependent on an object outside the body to sustain and support the being because of its premature condition at birth. *The result of this situation will be that the matrix of the mind, according to Freud—at least as I understand him—will be constituted by the meeting of the psychic representative by which, so to speak, being comes into existence through the demands of the ultimate reality of the body, and its association, a kind of instant co-option, with what the mind has kept as traces of former experiences (of satisfaction) that bear some similarity to the sought-for situation.* Most of the time this matrix is considered as not being formed of two parts, one coming from the innermost body—which, in fact, does not as such really know what it is seeking, only expecting some relief from the tension and pain that is experienced—and the contents provided by the mind which fit the demand. It may even be thought that it is only when the memory traces of the object meet with the urges of the body that meaning is found retrospectively. Usually psychoanalysts who find some value in such a model content themselves with the well-known "hallucinatory wish-fulfilment". They seem to overlook that they are dealing with the result of the process, mistaking it for the components of its origin: the move of the wish reproduces the move of the body stimuli seeking satisfaction and the awakening of the memory traces during the movement, reproducing the attempt to call for the object that once brought satisfaction.

If we consider this co-option that I infer between the psychic representative and the ideational representative, we realize why our conception of representation cannot be compared to the conceptions of the philosophers: because the philosophers conceive of them outside any situation of dependence towards the body and the object. What they seek in representation is what is permanent, immutable, and defined mainly in terms of its adequacy to reality—that is, through perception—a relation that in Freud is only a secondary one. They refer to the most tranquil, the quietest, and the most stable representations, because they include them in a chain going from perception to conception, whereas our concept of the representation is a dynamic one. It is dynamic because it deals with tensions, trying to resolve, through a modification directed both internally and externally, and calling for solutions according to the memory of the successful outcomes of the past, which have been kept, but that still do not master the devices to make them happen in a general state of urge, threat, and sometimes helplessness. The consequence of this is that the most primitive kind of mental activity in Freud labelled as instinctive refers to puzzling problems felt as experience in the body, requiring to be solved by something outside the body, with only a hazy intuition of what the answer could be to this relationship between what is internal and what is external. According to such a view, the concept of representation would expand in this vast field from the body to language. Representation would be closely associated with the psychic and with interpretation, the interpretation of the movement borne in the body by the young being, and interpretation about the need-satisfying object that is in the mind and altogether outside it. It is the meeting of these two types of interpretation that will culminate in the awareness of the relationship between subject and object. The subject is seen as the restless moving entity in quest of rest and having to cope with the multiple conditions of the object, aiming at their coexistence within him.

If there is no activity of interpretation, I cannot understand how any living organism belonging to the human species could survive. We can see from these remarks that the internal object is not a reproduction or a photocopy of the external object but a true creation. Needless to say, we have to make a distinction between the internal conscious representation of the external object, born through perception (whose structure is supposed to be more approximately that of the external object, and the internal unconscious representation of the external object), framed by the projections of sexuality, their frustrations and repression, and built up with the help of desire. This latter structure is the by-product of the imaginary work done on both the wishful object in relationship with the instinctual impulses, the desire of the subject, and the memory traces of the need-satisfying object—all of which are transformed and give birth to the representation of the object. They combine to form the unconscious thing-presentation. From that first reunion between the psychic representative coming from the body and of the memory traces of the image of the object, a new entity is created: the object representation. In this new mixture, the subject has worked out all his subjectivity not only because of the projection, but also because of something that stems from the inner sense of his body feeling to which he has given a conceivable form. It could be considered in terms of projection, if one emphasizes that it is above all a projection towards oneself, giving the opportunity to bring it back in the mind, when communicated to someone else, as an interpretation that may find some room in a wider context. Without solving all the problems regarding the hypothetical nature of the primitive kind of mental activity (mentioned by Freud in the Wolf Man, 1918b) I think that these ideas may help to throw some light on it.

At first sight, we would be tempted to interpret what he says as relating to a sort of intuition. If I am right in my construction of the matrix of the mind, we may assume that the participation of the body, from the point of view of what will become its instinctual impulses, favours the anticipation of more elaborate rational conceptions precisely because of its linking with the ideational representative and the future transformations of this amalgam. This association does not limit itself to providing answers about the state of immaturity of the child and his dependence on his parents. Whilst doing this, it inevitably fosters an intense fantasizing activity. Also, when it approaches reality, perception is inhabited by the contents that have inhabited the mind and found shelter in the internal world. Projection is at play, but, as Winnicott has shown beautifully, the mind finds and creates the objects simultaneously. And in this interaction of processes, where perception and projections combine, some mutual grasping between what is perceived and what is apprehended with an internal look can meet to form a kind of pattern, which, though very far from the real situation, has a suggestive power of evocation and generation of other forms in the mind—perhaps something analogous to what occurs in a squiggle game. We have a clearer view of a comparable process at a higher level of mental functioning with the sexual theories of children. It is as if we are tracing back their precursors as the first form of the subject's imprint on the matter of the events that happen to him.

We have witnessed a lot of controversy as to the relative importance of the internal object or the external, in the debates between Melanie Klein and Anna Freud, and the quarrel is not over. The baton has been taken up by Heinz Hartmann, who fought along the same lines as Anna Freud, but very differently. Then came Wilfred Bion following on the line of Mrs Klein. In fact Bion's work can also be considered as very different from its source of inspiration, as it includes a rehabilitation of some of Freud's hypotheses in a Kleinian framework. This applies to his ideas about thought processes. Happily enough this duel gave birth to a third issue, Donald Winnicott, who refused to be caught in the dichotomy between internal and external and grounded himself in the transitional space. Again, thirdness was the right solution, because it is true that the analytic space is under the sole sovereignty neither of the internal nor of the external world. But the whole dispute, at least as I see it, was in fact about the question of representation. Though Melanie Klein does not make much use of the notion, the question is: what stands between the sometimes irrepresentable matter of our deepest inner reality and the representation of realities through perception? Even in this last instance Freud later discovered, through disavowal, that perception could not be considered appropriate evidence for the access to reality. You remember that he had to postulate reality-testing earlier. Afterwards the interpretation of reality was dependent on the judgement of existence. He finally articulated the interpretation of the mental events according to two types of judgements: the judgement of attribution, which governs the pleasure–unpleasure principle, and the judgement of existence, which has to decide whether an object does or does not exist in reality, as in the reality principle.

Coming back to Peirce, we now have to consider his ideas about representation, as he has stated them, with what he has called the *representamen*. Let me remind you about some aspects of his position, which I have already outlined. Peirce said that thirdness is about what brings a first (a sign) into a second (its object) and the interpreting thought, which is itself a sign. Something similar has been said by the French linguist Benveniste about the third person in language (Benveniste, 1967). He defines it by a function of representation which is able to replace some parts of the statement and even an entire statement with a more manageable substitute. It should be noted that the operation of substitution seems to obey a process of internalization that acquires a specific function within a process that may be characterized itself—at least along Freudian views—as acting in the same way: word-presentations as substitutes for thing-presentations. These word-presentations, Freud thinks, are themselves devices to provide a quality to thoughts in order to enable us to perceive them. They can be said to stand between two systems trying to serve as intermediaries between the inner representation of objects and the communication of thoughts. But in the case of the third person, what seems to be emphasized here is the general extension of substitution and its possibility to be associated with any object reference, acquiring the function of being reflexive with the agency of discourse. Let us come back to Peirce. It appears to me that the essential function of a sign is to make inefficient relations efficient—not to set them into action but rather to establish a habit or general rule whereby they will act occasionally. If you think of that definition, in terms of efficiency or inefficiency dissociated from action, then you may think of what happens during the dream. Also, when the organization of signs leads to action, uncontrolled actions can occur as in parapraxes, or in acting out, or may induce others to act in the way you wish for your own self, or even to provoke acts that you would want to perform yourself. Peirce concluded that he needed a theory of representation, a position that brings him very close to Freud. He created a new concept—the *representamen*—to which I shall now come.

Interpretation is not limited to the communication of the analyst to the patient. One can say that everything that is conveyed to the analyst has undergone some kind of interpretation (unconscious, of course) by the patient before being communicated. This is obvious with the example of the dream. Though complex, these remarks help us to understand what we do when we analyse. There are signs—the words of patients or, in Freud's terms, word-presentations—and there are no objects. Objects are what words refer to or, in Freud's terms, things. Objects have a double existence: internal and external. Representations help us to make these two aspects communicate. But it is through the system of signs that we can connect the thought processes that account for their organization. Thus far, however, we have only talked about secondness and firstness. To be able to analyse is to refer to a third category: that of interpreting thought, which is itself a sign, though not evidently noticeable and which I call the tertiary processes. I consider these as constituting the mode of being of the sign, as (were it not so) words would not enable us to interpret. As Peirce says, an interpretant can be taken in such a vast sense that its interpretation is not necessarily a thought, but may occasionally be an action or an experience or a feeling. This is one of the most striking aspects of Peirce's theory—to extend the field of interpretation beyond language, particularly since he is a semiotician and not a linguist. In my view, the interpreting thought is not only present in word-presentation (i.e. in language) but also in object presentation. That is implied by Freud's conception of the unconscious. For instance, consider what Freud mentioned about the repressed as being attracted to what has already been repressed. Unconscious object representations are thus necessarily structured so as to possess the capacity of interpreting thought. In the same way, Freud underlines the fact that thought is mainly unconscious and thus, by implication, not dependent on words. Unconscious processes are capable of a certain type of thought different from secondary processes—interpretations—as can be seen in projection and projective identification. These are ways of thinking too, and therefore there is no need for Lacan to speak of the unconscious as structured like a language, because what matters is not a theory of the relationship of the subject to the signifier, but a theory of the relationship of the subject to a whole range of representations of different natures, where the signifier has a heterogeneous structure implying transformation when one passes from one type to another (i.e. dreams, fantasies, transference). I need now to clarify the difference between representation, sign, and *representamen*.

A sign, Peirce says, is probably everything that can be said about an object, but a *representamen* is everything that is subject to analysis in the mind. The sign is the association—the manifold association—with our associated thanks to the interpretant. For instance, with an object, the *representamen* is only what you can analyse from the relationship between firstness and secondness. Every sign stands for an object independent of itself, but it can only be a sign of that object insofar as that object is in and of itself the nature of a sign or thought. The sign does not affect the object but is affected by it, so that the object must be able to convey thought; every thought is a sign.

Of course, such a statement brings me to the conclusion that, for instance, any attempt at so-called dual relationships is a total illusion. I would say there is all the thickness of developing thought between the sign and what can be said through an analyst referred to as a subject or *representamen*. A representation is the operation of a sign or its relationship to an object, and this includes the possibility—essential when thinking about analysis—that it may be a word or any other material of the mind that is susceptible to be associated to other elements in a way that makes it possible to propose a meaning to this association. This statement is close to Lacan's concept of the symbolic. But the difference is that Lacan discarded the semiotic approach of Peirce because he believed that Saussure's conception of the unconscious structure of language would fit psychoanalysis better. There cannot be any subject if not for another subject, and a sign is whatever communicates a definite notion of an object by any means. But what for? "A *representamen* is the subject of a triadic relation with a second, called its object, and a third, called its interpretant. This triadic relationship being such that the *representamen* determines its interpretant to stand in the same triadic relation to the same object for any interpretant" (Peirce, 1931). I am quite aware that I am quoting very difficult statements, but this is a fundamental point. On the other hand, this is a conceptual structure that does justice to the complexity of the act of interpretation in analysis. Interpretation is surely the core of analytic action, and I prefer to have to ponder these dense statements rather than oversimplify the whole thing by adopting a schematic attitude.

If we now come back to the concept of the psyche, the inaugural moment of thought is the meeting of the unrepresentable, the psychic representative expressing the bodily demand, and the cathexis of a memory trace left by the object. From this original binding, the possibility of analytic work through transference is opened up. To put it very schematically, the psyche is the effect of the relationship of two bodies, one of them being absent. Let me try to explain what I understood from Peirce's hypothesis. The idea of a *representamen* tries to define a process more than a condition, as in the relationship to perception. We find here an analogy with Freud's concept of representation, which as we have seen reproduces and reshapes itself very clearly with the double standard of things and words to which he adds this very different kind of representation of messages borne in the body and having to find some expression when they reach the mind. Of course, Peirce does not bother directly about that. But when he assumes that an interpretative thought can be found in a feeling or in action, he opens up the possibility of also including messages from the body. It is this set of transformations that one has to keep in mind. Peirce focuses his elaboration along several lines. The first one conceives the sign as the manifestation of the *representance* by its capacity to establish a relationship of some kind, or at any rate in which substitution is at play. He remains vague as to the limits of what the relationship is about. He assumes at this stage that the sign is "something that stands for". In this process where a relationship leads to a substitution we can think of an analogy: what Freud describes in the dream work. No subject is involved here: the psyche is reduced to the operation by which it transforms contents through condensation and displacement. Of course the difference between Freud and Peirce is the hypothesis in the former of the pleasure–unpleasure principle which accounts for the attempt of the realization of a wish in the dream. But in both cases what is important is the result: the capacity to establish a relationship that includes the replacement of an original statement by something else acting as a substitute. We can also think of the object presentations that are less a translation of the perception of the object than a relationship between impressions derived from sense impressions left by the object, standing as a substitution for it.

The change comes from the communication of this first relationship. What was labelled as *something* undergoes a considerable change when communicated to *someone*. What happens is the pursuit of the process of representation within a person or in another person. Here it is not a mere relationship that occurs but a *creation* either of an equivalent sign (the substitution does not go beyond a similar sign) or a new mental event, the occurrence of a more developed sign. How can this happen if not by taking "something" of the proposed sign and including it in a more extensive set of associations. It is there that Peirce introduces the interpretant. We can deduce that an interpretant is what changes an already existing relationship with the action of a subject. I am not sure that we need to consider the *someone* as always referring to another person. We can just as well understand this phase as the operation of thinking in a secondary approach, not because it comes after the first, but because it examines an already existing relationship limited to a process of substitution. The specificity of the interpretant is said to stand for something of its object. We witness here the return of the term *something* which we could have thought as having disappeared with the outcome of the address to someone. In fact, Peirce wants to define the matter on which the mind has to work. After the intervention of the interpretant, the transformations that have occurred with the development of a higher type of sign are confronted anew with the matter that they can reshape in this new approach. This is how *something* is back, which will need further elaboration. What is now new is no longer related to the operation of the relationship, it is related to what Peirce qualifies as *something of its object*. Here is an ambiguity. Does he mean the object on which the sign has worked to form the relationship? Or does he mean that the object is the outcome of the relationship itself, i.e. the meaning that can be drawn from the intrapsychic relationship? It is possible that the two meanings combine, but the important thing to understand is that the reference to the object is mentioned in the theory only after the intervention of the subject— either as some other person or as the person's own. The object would not exist empirically outside the mental events that allow some relationship to appear. It is always indirectly apprehended. This also looks close to Freud's theory. Object and interpretant are associated by the process of substitution, itself submitted to a substitution of another type including a subject. This reminds me of Freud defining secondary processes as being able to express relationships of relationships. Peirce has no other way to define what he considers to be the "foundation of *representamen*" as an idea.

Here he is obliged to come back to traditional philosophical thinking. But what matters for us is the way the triadic relationship keeps moving forward. The *representamen* determines its interpretant to stand in the same triadic relation to the same object for any interpretant.

In thirdness there is always one term that is disturbing by being undesirable or unwanted, or one missing term that would change the triangular structure to form two pairs. We can now see that the nature of the psyche is linked not only with the unconscious but also with the parents. This is with a whole range of psychic qualities—conscious, preconscious, and unconscious— and also with the second *topographic model, which increases the heterogeneity of the agencies of the psychic apparatus, each one following different modalities of treating the information related to internal needs, or about the external world, or having to submit to drastic suppression in the mind. I am here mentioning the three parts of the psychic apparatus: id, ego, and superego.* On these three agencies, we can superimpose three figures if we want, in order to make them come alive. If we want an image of them, we can assign the relationship with the mother to her mother, as one of helping the building-up of the ego. You may protest that mothers fulfil superego functions and fathers id functions; but, by and large, this statement is true, and it is largely nature's fault, not ours. The superego quality of fatherhood is not due to any inherent superiority of men over women but, rather, to do with the regrettable limitation that fathers cannot bear children. They do not know what it means to be two in one, to feed a baby, nor to feel its flesh as their flesh. This is the crux of the matter: that one day this paradise has to come to an end, that two in one becomes two who are kept apart, and this is why a third is needed. We can now propose another view to Peirce's idea according to psychoanalysis. Firstness is being, secondness relating, and thirdness thinking. Thirdness is also a condition of time. If the unconscious ignores time, we know that the Oedipus complex deals not only with the difference of the sexes but also with the difference of generations. Two generations are not enough to define someone. It could be objected, for instance, that this conception of thirdness lacks a very important dimension, that of conflict, but I do not think that this is justified. As Peirce says, everything that comes before the mind contains an element of struggle, and this is present even in rudimentary fragments of an experience such as a simple feeling, because such a feeling always has a degree of vividness and diffusion and always stands in reaction to other feelings. This is the basic condition of how they appear in the mind: never isolated but as part of sets that include opposition. The simplest feature of what is present in the mind is the element of struggle: the mutual action of two things without reference to a third nor to any mediation, nor without consideration of the law of action (Peirce). If, in the endeavour to find some idea that does not involve the elements of struggle, we imagine a universe that consists of a single quality that never changes, there must still be some degree of steadiness in this imagining, or else we could not ask whether there was an object that has any positive substance. Peirce claims that this steadiness consists in the fact that if our mental manipulation is delicate enough, the hypothesis will resist the change. I think it is a beautiful way of presenting things and to show that the psychic activity is also a time of living. The preceding remarks relate to secondness, which has to deal with the outcome of changes in being, as a result of the influence of force (action and reaction). Behind this we find the idea of coupling, even between remote subjects. This coupling is limited to these two subjects exclusively. It is a constant duality.

We have to come more precisely to thirdness. Peirce developed the idea in the context of a logic of relatives opposing it to firstness and secondness. Thirdness is the highest capacity of the mind. He gave different versions of it. He thought of it as modifications of the being of a subject which is a mode of a second in the measure that is a modification of a third. We can think here that this would be a simple extension of secondness. In fact, there is a change of order, because it is only there that meaning, understanding, and generalizations are possible. This is a requisite to the formulation of a law. But the outcome of thirdness needs to have primarity and secondness independently fixed, otherwise thirdness would lack a basis for its operations. Peirce gave another statement about it, different from the preceding. He used the comparison of an individual within a system. He says that if there is a relationship within which each individual in the system stands bearing a relationship to any other, but in which no third stands in connection with the last other, then, in relation to each individual of the system, any other individual stands in that relationship (Peirce, 1931, Vol. I, Book 2: 5.1). This characterizes finished multitudes. Here, the third is not in an immediate connection with the second, but spreads all over the system and finds its application in any example of secondness. In summary, primariness has to do with sensations, feelings, and qualities; secondness with the modifications being undergone with external forces; and thirdness with what Peirce considers the ground of generalization and continuity. Peirce warns us against the temptation of oversimplifying the conception of the relationships between these categories. We need not suppose that the qualities of firstness emerged as separate entities that related to the others afterwards. The state of affairs is exactly opposite to this. The general and independent potentiality has become limited and heterogeneous. This is a powerful indication that we should not think of this logic of relationships as obeying the schematic patterns of the child's development. Peirce has hesitated to find the points that characterize thirdness; he considered two uses—mediation and representation—but he was afraid to extend abusively the usual meaning of this last word.

The *representamen* seems to extend to the whole definition altogether, and more specifically to the subject, because it is a subject whose attribute is to bring forward its capacity of interpreting the relationship between subject and object. There is no understanding of such a relationship which would do away with interpretation. But moreover, to interpret is not only to assess or to give meaning, it is also, through its very exercise (acting as a third factor), to demonstrate the possibility of proceeding to a substitution of the subject by the interpretant and to go on in the process in such a way that the interpretant would play this role for any other interpretant. Here, it seems to me, is an essential finding: the connection of interpretations, together with substitution and dynamics. The relationship between subject and object has not only to be transformed by the operation of an interpretant, it opens up the field of interpretation applying it to any other interpretant. How important these hypotheses could be for psychoanalysis! The first consequence is that an exclusive reference to the relationship between a subject and an object (usually called "object relationship") is insufficient and, in my view, wrong. If we add, with Peirce, the category of the interpretant (distinct from the category of the subject), we suggest that with this notion—the interpretant—there will come into play a specific function. Its task will be to extend and to generalize the outcome of the relation between subject and object in a particular experience. This is how I understand Peirce's definition, which speaks of the application for "any other interpretant". This is not to be confused with "any other subject", as it is within the discourse of the subject that the interpretant is linked to other interpretants. This is the basic idea that more than two parties are necessary to categorize and generalize the exchanges of a relationship. This three-party relationship is the matrix of the mind. Therefore, a dual relationship will not do, as it does not do justice to the complexity of the process of communication in terms of thought processes. This reminds me of Bion's distinction between thoughts and thinking, which needs an apparatus to transform the thoughts. In other words, the representation is about the representation of a relationship, rather than one about the different elements that took part in it. Interpretants are not persons, they are signs and characterize the mode of being a sign. What is important to emphasize is the solidarity between subject–interpretant–representation. Not only does the interpretant act in a way that makes it indissociable to meaning, and not only does its mediating quality serve as a link in the relationship with an object, but also, and even more, it serves to ensure continuity because of its potentiality of reproducing the relationship that now stands in the place of the subject for any other interpretant. If we do not take notice of this operation, we shall not be able to find any explanation for the process of interpretation in the analytic setting, considering that what the analyst interprets from the patient's material is what has been interpreted by the analysand both in his internal world and in the way it is communicated to this other object: the analyst.

Thought is the manipulation of signs. Thinking does not exist apart from the signs through which it expresses itself. This capacity of thought opens the way for an infinite system of interpretation. Here, I think we are closer to Freud than with any other philosopher. Peirce's logic of relatives applies to what is psychic. If we want to apply them to our problems of development we should try to see how they can coexist in the different periods rather than stem from one to another. True knowledge has to give up the idea that the understanding of the primitive stages will give the key to more advanced modes of thinking. It is only through thirdness that we can have the possibility of understanding the relationship of the mind—maybe because no matter how archaic a transference relationship can appear, as it happens in the analytic relationship it cannot be labelled any more as purely archaic but more as a reorganization of what is supposed to evoke archaicity and is nevertheless intelligible to the mind of the analyst (which it would not be if it were only archaic). The analysis of a dream shows that, not only in its telling but also in what we assume to be the dream work, a form of thirdness is present, allowing it to be interpretable. At any age, psychoanalytic treatments are all based on interpretation. Even when dealing with the so-called dual relationship? It is through interpretation that the situation can be modified. In the so-called dual relationship there must be some connections within thirdness, which can be heard by the patient, as young as he may be or as regressed as he is. That must encourage us to carry our research forward in that direction instead of believing in simplistic explanations. I assume that Winnicott's ideas on the location of cultural experience could be seen in the light of some of these ideas. Bion—or, to be more precise, Keats, quoted by Bion—talked about negative capability as the ability to tolerate mystery and doubt and as a quality required for being an analyst. Also, one should mention here Winnicott's potential space, which can hardly be observed but only reached through imagination. Lacan, too, emphasized the role of language in terms of presence and absence. All of these ideas, whether derived from Bion, Winnicott, or Lacan—or, indeed, from developments of Freud's conception or representation—use absence as the precondition for representation. Otherwise, perception comes into play, but things are probably not so simple, even in perception, since this too involves representation operating beyond ordinary awareness.

I hope that I have succeeded in showing that the nature of the psychic can never be reduced to a dual relationship. Although I am not so immodest as to credit myself with such a discovery, I know where I stand and where my thinking is grounded. I am also convinced that many others are fighting for a different conception of psychoanalysis and that metaphors are sometimes dangerous as supporting illusions. For myself, I find it an illusion to believe that one can grasp the nature of the psychic without the third element, which carries with it an inevitable metaphoric dimension.

FOUR

The posthumous Winnicott: on *Human Nature*

Winnicott and myself have at least one point in common: we enjoy lecturing. Clare Winnicott tells us that her husband, Donald W. Winnicott, was invited in 1936 by Susannah Isaacs to lecture to teachers and professors (Winnicott, 1988). After the war, he resumed the lectures from 1954 until 1971. His lectures were well attended because he would express himself with spontaneity which made them attractive. He subsequently tried to compile a book of the lectures, starting in 1954, and there were two synopses. One was written in 1954 and a second in 1967, but he never succeeded in providing a final version and completing the book. So, the posthumously published book, *Human Nature* (1988), could be described as the fragments of an unfinished symphony. We know that some of the works of a creator which have remained in a preparatory phase can teach us a lot compared to those that have reached maturity and publication. We can compare it to Freud's *Outline of Psychoanalysis* (1940a [1938]), which is

---

This *Squiggle* Public Lecture was presented on 29 June 1996 at Regents College in celebration of D. W. Winnicott's Centenary year.

also unfinished, though it was left incomplete because of Freud's death.

Because so much has been published on Winnicott's writings, it seemed to me that an original way of celebrating his memory was to comment on the unwritten Winnicott. As Henry James (an author Winnicott read during World War I) said: "The pearl is the unwritten." In fact, here we are dealing with the unpublished rather than the unwritten. But to some extent the unpublished amounts to the unwritten—or let us say we have here a *transitional writing* between the unsaid and the published. Therefore, the book as it stands both is and is not the text.

Two conclusions came to me after my reading of *Human Nature*. The first was how Donald W. Winnicott's recapitulation was in continuation with Freud's work. The author did not break off with Freud but rather completed his work. The second was how much of an independent thinker Winnicott was. He was the true leader of the independent stream in the British Psycho-Analytical Society. This is why he is a formidable thinker. *Human Nature* is a classical concept of philosophy. Today it raises many reservations among philosophers because it implies a fixed, rigid concept of the nature of man, as if it could be grasped out of any historical context. Let us go back to it, in order to ascertain the point at which Winnicott began. The *concept of human nature* implies an opposition between the aims and goals of *man's specific nature*, which is cultural (arts, sciences, ethics, religion), and the goals and aims of his *animal nature*, that is, to say his *natural nature*. Freud's work stands in the middle of the two; it theoretically describes the ontogenesis of man from birth to adulthood, from id to superego. The implication is also of an area linked with biology, which to some extent may coincide with what is inherited in the child whose evolution will either add to it (epigenesis) or deeply modify it, mixing so tightly the innate and the acquired in such a way that they become hardly distinguishable. The philosophical definition of nature refers to *the principle that is supposed to produce the development of a being, which realizes a certain type* (Lalande, 1968). There is implicit reference here to Aristotle, Bacon, and Descartes. *Nature is the native condition of man* (in opposition to God's revelation, or grace, or civilization). Here there is a contradiction—nature is understood as implying either a set of laws and rules or as synonymous with chaos. Maybe Winnicott was inspired by John Stuart Mill's *Essay on Nature* (1874). Anyhow, the term has so many meanings that it is self-contradictory—I would add—*just as human nature is*.

Our task is not a philosophical one (even if it cannot avoid leaning on philosophy to know the meaning of the terms we use to define it); it is about analysing people: children and children no longer (Paula Heimann, 1989). In his preface, Winnicott reminds us that an analyst analyses about 70 patients during the course of his career. To draw conclusions on human nature on the basis of 70 patients is an audacious endeavour. On the other hand, nobody has ever tried to understand so many people so deeply and thoroughly as the psychoanalyst. Though the author insists on his paediatric background and emphasizes the continuity between paediatrics, child psychiatry, adult psychiatry, and, finally, psychoanalysis (child and adult), I will mention here an important statement with which I am in total agreement.

> At about this time I was also gradually lured into the treatment of the more psychotic type of adult patient, and I found that I could learn much about the psychology of early infancy from adults who were deeply regressed in the course of psychoanalytic treatment; much of which could not be learned by direct observation of infants, nor from the analyses even of children of two and a half years. This psychoanalytic work with adults of a psychotic type proved extremely exacting and time-absorbing and by no means always obviously successful. In one case which ended tragically, I gave 2,500 hours of my professional life, without hope of remuneration. Nevertheless, this work taught me more than any other kind. [*Human Nature*, p. 50]

It is refreshing to read these lines when I think of the present brainwashing about direct child observation. The book, *Human Nature*, is so rich and so full of implications that I will select only a *few* of the problems with which Winnicott wanted to deal. And it is interesting to note that all of them are not mentioned elsewhere in his work. Some statements are surprising—for example his recognition of the importance of the drives. Before entering into the questions I have selected, I would like to emphasize one point, which is probably obvious to you but not to me: the accent on *emotional development*. This is a common paradigm to British psychoanalysis in general. It is not so firmly stated by North American psychoanalysts, who would insist, rather, on the ego (a very tricky concept), and certainly not by the analysts on the other side of the channel, who will turn, according to their preferences, to the drives or to the signifier. Winnicott and Bion place emotional development and emotional experience at the beginning (or, as Adam Phillips, 1988, says on Winnicott—quoting T. S. Eliot—at the end, probably meaning the major goal): in other words, at the beginning or at the centre, depending on whether you are developmentally or structurally minded. This is very clearly stated in the Introduction to Part IV, "From Instinct Theory to Ego Theory":

> Somewhat artificially I shall choose three different languages for the description of the earlier phenomena of emotional development. First I shall discuss
> a. the establishment of a relationship with external reality;
> b. the integration of the unit self from an unintegrated state;
> c. the lodgement of the psyche in the body.
>
> I can find no clear sequence in development that can be used to determine the order of description. [*Human Nature*, p. 99]

It is interesting to note that Winnicott refers here to a paper written in 1945—very early on in his work. The sequence he describes can be used as the main idea guiding his thought. We can note here:

- the primitive importance of external reality;
- the guideline orientation: unintegrated state of the unit to the Self;
- the psyche as embodied in the body.

One can see immediately Winnicott's originality as different from that of the Freuds (Sigmund and Anna) or the Kleinians (Melanie and others). There is a prophetic Winnicott in this book. At the end of the Introduction to Part I he states:

> I long for this day [the recognition of child psychiatry], and have longed for it throughout three decades. But the danger is that the painful side of the new development will be avoided, and an attempt will be made to find a way round; theories

will be reformulated, implying that psychiatric disorder is a product not of emotional conflict but of heredity, constitution, endocrine imbalance, and crude mismanagement. [*Human Nature*, p. 10]

At the time Winnicott could not have known about neurosciences or cognitive sciences. If the words were still lacking, the thing was already there. It was an anticipation, but it was based on the inevitability of regression after an unbearable advance had been made in thought. It is not surprising that the attacks are now focused on Freud in the United States.

I propose to comment on the following points:

1. the distinctions between psyche–soma, soul, mind, intellect;
2. instinct theory, sexuality, aggression, and the death instinct;
3. the Oedipus complex;
4. object relations theory;
5. reality, internal and external.

You will certainly understand that it is only possible to make a survey of this vast and unachieved totality. One wonders what other questions Winnicott would have encompassed if he had managed to finish writing what he wanted to say.

Psyche–soma, soul, mind, intellect

Reading *Human Nature*, one is struck by the importance of psychosomatics in Winnicott's work. He deals with it at length in the first part and ends the book with a chapter entitled "Psychosomatic Disorder Reconsidered". This indicates that *emotional development* as a paradigm implies a preliminary postulate: emotions that play an essential part of the human psyche are rooted in the body (just as Freud thought that instincts represented the roots of the psyche in the somatic). Therefore, the importance of the concept of, I shall say, *incarnation* (which rejects the objection that *psychoanalysis* is synonymous with *psychogenesis* and dis-incarnation) accepts the fact that somatic problems in the early phases of life are an important factor of psychic development. In Chapter III of Part IV, he provides interesting views on the *dwelling* of the psyche in the body. He seems to have foreseen Didier Anzieu's concept of the skin-ego, which can be traced as playing a role in *borderline personality disorders* (Anzieu, 1985). Moreover he states:

> There is a psychotic anxiety underlying psychosomatic disorder even though in many cases at more superficial levels there can be clearly shown to be hypochondriacal or neurotic factors. [*Human Nature*, p. 8]

It is my belief that the relationship between psychosis and psychosomatosis is a promising field of research, as the Paris Psychosomatics School led by the late Pierre Marty has started to investigate. It is here that the concept of integration is important to Winnicott's distinction between unintegration—the state supposed to exist at birth—and disintegration, which is the result of regression (Winnicott, 1962). It is impossible in my view to dissociate this concept of the psyche–soma relationship from Freud's concept of instinct, "a concept at the limit of the somatic and the psychic".

Here is a double difference: a difference between the somatic and the psychic (united and separated as such) and a difference between the Self and the environment. I shall *locate the Self as standing between the body and the external world—i.e. the other*. The psyche is an intermediate structure between the organism and the environment. Further distinctions are needed between organism and soma on one side, and self, environment, and Other on the other side. Here it is less a question of opposing the "deeper inside" to the "farther outside", than to distinguish the Self as an immediate experience bordered with *two other outsides*, one in the depth of the body, the second beyond its limits in the world. Freud already said that the id was the second external world to the ego. An important idea is presented now: "The gathering together of the self constitutes an act of hostility to the not-Me..." (*Human Nature*, p. 124). Our unity is based on a paranoid trend, just as the unity of groups or societies or nations implies an underlying paranoia towards other groups, societies, or nations. Think of Euro '96. No need to mention mad cows here, as madness is more widely spread to other domains.

We can now see what the *soul* is for Winnicott: an attribute of the psyche seen as *the imaginative elaboration of body functioning*.

This implies normal functioning of the brain. As far as soul is concerned, it can be healthy or ill. Winnicott expects many objections. But if you read Macbeth, things will appear clearly. Shakespeare wrote the play to challenge James II, who was supposed to be an expert in theology. You can see that Macbeth's soul is sick but not his spirit, because the soul can be corrupted, probably because of its dependence on flesh. So we have to purify our soul, our spirit being kept safe by God. Health of the soul is incompatible with the voluntary damage (leucotomy) because a brain mutilated in order to improve behaviour cannot coexist with an access to sanity (*Human Nature*, p. 52). A very original point made by Winnicott is his concept of the *intellect*: "there is no meaning to the term intellectual health" (*Human Nature*, p. 12)—maybe because the intellect has no reference to the other. Intellect depends on brain functioning. It is evaluated quantitatively (Winnicott is referring to IQ) and can be affected by all sorts of physical injuries of the brain. Today we can think of the attempt of the cognitive sciences to get rid of psychoanalytic approaches. This means denying that our judgements are strongly influenced by factors rooted in our subjective, emotionally determined psychic activity, which is not synonymous with the intellect. The question is more complicated because, as Winnicott says:

> The psyche can be ill itself, that is to say distorted by emotional developmental failures, in spite of a healthy brain basis for its functioning. [*Human Nature*, p. 12]

Let's come now to the *mind*. "Mind" is a word that cannot be translated into French. We usually translate it as *"esprit"*, but this is inappropriate. Mind is not spirit. Winnicott says:

- The child's body belongs to the paediatrician
- The soul belongs to the minister of religion
- The psyche belongs to the dynamic psychologist
- The mind belongs to the philosopher. [*Human Nature*, p. 7]

In Chapter VII of *Human Nature*, Winnicott summarizes:

> At first, there is soma, then a psyche that in health gradually becomes anchored to the soma; sooner or later a third phenomenon appears which is called intellect or mind. [*Human Nature*, p. 139]

Let us note in passing that the anchorage of psyche to soma is secondary; it comes after the birth of the psyche as distinct from the soma.

Here again we see a difference with Freud's work. For the founder of psychoanalysis, everything starts from the body through its psychic primitive expression: the instincts. For Winnicott, this arrives as a second move. How can we imagine a psyche that is not rooted, from the beginning, in the body? I suggest that what Winnicott implied is that the two series, psyche and soma, are not united in the beginning. They have to accomplish this task, which is not a given but an achievement for the integration of the psyche–soma unit. In other words, the child has to take possession of the outcome of the relationship between himself and the mother. I suppose the idea explains the different dissociations that can take place, affecting the psyche–soma unit. I have spent some time on these ideas of Winnicott because they do not belong to the corpus of classical psychoanalytic theory, and seem to be more part of psychology or philosophy. It was interesting to recall them before coming to more familiar concepts such as instincts, objects, or the depressive position—to which I will now turn. I shall not go into too much detail because these topics are well known. I shall only underline Winnicott's originality, at least those aspects of it which are not so obvious in his other books.

Instinct theory, Oedipus complex, object relationships

The preceding ideas are born from Winnicott's own creativity. It is also interesting to point out how he interprets the findings of his predecessors. He is a successor to Freud and Melanie Klein, shaping their ideas in his own frame. For Winnicott, the mutative moment in a child's development occurs when he or she can achieve a capacity for concern—a characteristic of the psychoanalyst as a therapist. Winnicott does not hide the autobiographical origin of this concept, bearing in mind how he savagely destroyed a doll—his sister's—with his private croquet mallet (incidentally, the French word *croquer* means to bite or to draw). His father, witnessing the boy's despair after his deed, repaired the doll successfully. Here is an idea different from what is usually admitted: the manifestations of instinct can be tolerable if and only when the idea of reparation has been achieved in the child, indicating a developing capacity. So at the centre of human development is the depressive position, which leads to reparation and by extension to the capacity for concern. Before the depressive position is a stage of ruthless love. This is different from Freud and from Klein. Winnicott does not agree with either Freud's death instinct or with Klein's paranoid–schizoid position. On the other hand, one can establish parallels between ruthless love and primary narcissism. The capacity for concern implies the awareness of the existence of the object and some kind of care for its integrity. Winnicott emphasizes the importance of the distinction between the part object and the whole object. He states it in a very simple way, tracing a frontier before and after the two-year-old child. Winnicott's baby before two is not characterized, as by Freud, by the predominance of part instincts and erotogenic zones and autoeroticism, nor, as by Klein, by the paranoid–schizoid phase. For Winnicott it is the necessity to build up a Self, to cope with external reality, to try to achieve oneness, autonomy, self-awareness, and integration that is at the beginning. Aggression and destruction are the most debatable part of Freud's last theory of instincts. Since Freud there has been an increasing emphasis on both of them. In present psychoanalysis we have reached the point where aggression has completely overshadowed sexuality—which is not the case in *Human Nature*.

Winnicott's paper, "On the Use of an Object and Relating through Identifications" (1968), is quoted many times in this book. This paper shows that aggression can take place only by de-cathecting the object's existence without any kind of "bloodshed", if I may say so. Moreover, Madeleine Davis has shown that destruction in Winnicott's work had to be considered as an achievement. The words, "I am", thought Winnicott, "are the most dangerous words in the languages of the world" (Winnicott, 1986a, p. 141).

Winnicott mentioned the need for a term such as "life force", which is exactly what Freud meant by "life and love instincts". This view of destruction broadens our scope and considers it as not limited to the negative affects (jealousy, envy, anger, frustration). Aggression is necessary to discover the external world, and it is a condition for the achievement of the reality of the object as separate from the Self. Freud had already said in 1915 that the object was discovered in hatred. This assertion has been discussed at length but misunderstood. Otherwise we have eternal fusion, which is non-separateness. Madeleine Davis writes profoundly that "Destruction becomes the unconscious backcloth for love of a real object" (Davis, 1985). It is important to experience it, the object being outside the area of omnipotent control. In *Human Nature*, Winnicott gives an account, never so complete and so deeply thought about as here, of instinct theory. Lots of questions arise from his exposition. How to match the descriptions of development from the point of view of instinct theory and from the point of view of the development of self and object? Maybe these unanswered questions prevented Winnicott from ending the book and publishing it. Maybe some other reasons were the cause of his giving up.

I will take the opportunity to emphasize some neglected issues in Winnicott's work. Contrary to current opinion, Winnicott cannot be classified as an unconditional representative of object relations theory. Madeleine Davis has shown this very convincingly. He is halfway between Freud and Klein from this point of view. Madeleine Davis insists on Darwin's influence, suggesting the presence of an evolutionary view in Winnicott (Davis & Wallbridge, 1981). Another way of demonstrating his agreement with Freud's basic hypothesis is his acceptance of primary narcissism—a point that distinguishes his concepts from those of Fairbairn, of Klein, and of Balint. Being myself a defender of the existence of primary narcissism, I was quite happy to notice our agreement on this. Moreover, instead of criticizing instinct theory, Winnicott thinks highly of it:

> Instinct-freedom promotes body health, and from this it follows that in normal development with increasing instinct control, the body has to be sacrificed at many points.... [*Human Nature*, p. 24]

False self organization largely depends on instinct control personally acquired, or through the mother's denial or non-acceptance of its manifestations in her child. An important distinction needs to be made between infant care and instinct functioning in child development.

> If (in one case) the accent is on *integration through good infant care*, the personality may be well founded. If the accent is on integration through *impulse and instinctual experience* and through the anger that maintains its relation to desire, then the personality is likely to be interesting, even exciting in quality. In health there is enough of each of these two, and the combination of the two spells stability. When there is not enough of either, integration is never well established, or is established in a set way, overemphasised and heavily defended, and allowing of no relaxation, restful integration. [*Human Nature*, p. 120]

About impulse and instinct experience leading to the Oedipus complex

Winnicott observes that this relationship leads to a paradoxical statement. The Oedipus complex is seen as the achievement of health (relationships involving persons). Winnicott sees castration anxiety as a blessing, as it enables earlier anxiety to follow a path other than that of impotent agony:

> Almost every aspect of relationships between whole persons was touched on by Freud himself, and in fact it is very difficult now to contribute, except by a fresh statement of what is accepted. Freud did the unpleasant things for us, pointing out the reality and force of the unconscious, getting to the pain, anguish, and conflict which invariably lie at the root of symptom formations. He also put forward (arrogantly it could be seen) the importance of instinct and the significance of childhood sexuality. Any theory that denies or bypasses these matters is unhelpful. [*Human Nature*, p. 36]

Winnicott has frequently been accused of understating the role of the father—not by the Kleinians, of course, more by the French Freudians. At the end of his life, Winnicott said that it was only with the father that the child could really achieve separation from the mother. This is true. In fact, before anything else, the father is the one to separate the child from the mother. Castration anxiety is bound up with the fear that, without a penis, a reunification with the mother is no longer possible, as Ferenczi said. The ambiguity of the father figure as both separator and castrator, as well as the barrier against pathological symbiosis, with paranoid anxieties experienced in a state of helplessness and despair, show that the relationship of the child to the father is not, by any means, less complicated than with the mother.

Imaginative elaboration, fantasy, transitional phenomena

It is of importance to underline that for Winnicott, just as for Freud, the main basis for emotional development and the building of the psyche is *fantasy*, or, as he calls it, *imaginative elaboration*. "The psyche begins as an imaginative elaboration of physical functioning" (*Human Nature*, p. 19). To put things differently I shall say that imaginative elaboration is very much linked with absence. I have said elsewhere that the psyche was the relationship between two bodies, one of them being absent. The originality of Winnicott's contribution to this problem is that he opened a way to the traditional dilemma of putting the emphasis on absence or conversely on presence. What he did was to consider—once again—the point between reunion (presence) and separation (absence). He showed how at the moment preceding reunion (or full presence in encounter), the object was created just as the moment of separation (the start of absence) could be used further as a space of potential reunion. This view enriched the theory of symbolism, giving a dynamic view of it, emphasizing the moment during which the parts were separated or united again—therefore, the corollary: the object is found (as opposed to lost) and created (as opposed to perceived). This implies an entirely new view of the relationships between representation (i.e. memory) and perception (i.e. consciousness). We can see the importance of the chain of events from soma to thinking. An important distinction *not made by Winnicott* is between intellect and thinking. Here *Bion is helpful*. Thinking, in the way it differs from intellectualizing, is drawn from emotional experience, which means that the roots are in instinctual manifestations, growing into imaginative elaboration, i.e. fantasy relationship with reality. The created–found object is the result of the subjective object and the objectively perceived one.

I shall end my reading of *Human Nature* with Winnicott's most original contribution: transitional space and transitional phenomena. There is a close relationship between fantasy and the conception of the transitional object. Fantasy and the transitional object result from imaginative elaboration as a human characteristic. They are also related to the notion of psychic reality, if one keeps in mind that here we are talking about unconscious fantasies uncontrolled by consciousness. Winnicott's original approach is to help us understand the internal world in terms of chaos (a chaos caused by the predominance of instinct in the oral phase), which calls for some kind of order. It is time to remember how Winnicott has refused to be caught in the dilemma of inside or outside. Chaos is related not to unintegration, but to disintegration as a regressive phenomenon. In other words, chaos is not the state preceding order but the loss of an already established order, however minimal. Transitional phenomena appear as a result of separation. They belong to symbolization processes in their paradoxical logics (the object is and is not the breast, the breast is and is not the mother). I would include them in what I call tertiary processes as a go-between between primary and secondary processes; they are essential to psychoanalytic working through.

Since Winnicott, "illusion" is no longer a pejorative term—a fallacy that should not exist. It has become a useful concept to experience and to think about. It has not been sufficiently emphasized that there are close relationships between the instinct (better to use the term "drive"), imaginative elaboration, and illusion. How? Instincts or primary drives—as the word suggests—are expansions pushing forward [*Triebe*] and outside in order to accomplish an aim related to gratification (this is true for any instinctual aim, whether erotic or aggressive) towards an object that is located outside. This calls for the idea of emergence. Emergence comes from solitude and, before that, unaliveness, which is sometimes reached by extreme regression. I call it decathexis or disinvestment. In any case, instincts—the love or life instincts—are responsible for this *growth*, this "bud" of being: we sometimes use the expression *bud of instinct* to name some psychic processes such as hallucination. Instincts are at the root of the imaginative elaboration. They are a spring, a shoot, spontaneously grown up, and the working-through of a non-immediate or total gratification. And this is where we meet illusion. Winnicott uses the same description for illusion: an emergence, i.e. a growth out of solitude, with the purpose of achieving an aim. But he believes that illusion is prior to instinct. In the beginning is a pre-dependent aloneness. Illusion and emergence are necessarily associated with dependence—it sustains the omnipotence of having created the object.

> Where the complications are not too great, something very simple happens. It is difficult to find the right words to describe this simple event; but it can be said that by reason of an aliveness in the infant and through the development of instinct tension the infant comes to expect something; and then there is a reaching out which can soon take the form of an impulsive movement of the hand or a movement of the mouth towards a presumed object. I think it is not out of place to say that the infant is ready to be creative. [*Human Nature*, p. 102]

There is something extremely suggestive in Winnicott's theorization about the intermediary stage between primary narcissism and object relationships. The intermediary stage is presented as referring to a layer constituted of an aspect of the mother and an aspect of the baby. "It is mad to hold this view and yet the view must be maintained" (*Human Nature*, p. 157). He then speaks of a *set of substances* common to mother and child but has difficulty in saying where one ends and the other begins. The *madness* about such a notion relates to the point of development from primary narcissism to object relationships. A substance that joins and separates will be represented by the transitional objects.

Conclusion: philosophy and reality

I started with philosophy and shall end with it. Confronting idealistic and realistic concepts, Winnicott writes:

> I would put it this way. Some babies are fortunate enough to have a mother whose initial active adaptation to their infant's needs was good enough. This enables them to have the illusion of actually finding what was created (hallucinated).

Eventually, after a capacity for relationships has been established, such babies can take the next step towards recognition of the essential aloneness of the human being. Eventually such a baby grows up to say, "I know that there is no direct contact between external reality and myself, only an illusion of contact, a midway phenomenon that works very well for me when I am not tired. I couldn't care less that there is a philosophical problem involved."

Babies with slightly less fortunate experiences are really bothered by the idea of there being no direct contact with external reality. A sense of threat of loss of capacity for relationships hangs over them all the time. For them the philosophical problem becomes and remains a vital one, a matter of life and death, of feeding or starvation, of love or isolation. [*Human Nature*, pp. 114–115]

Healthy people, philosophers (mildly healthy or sometimes not healthy at all), schizoid people—where does Winnicott stand? We do not know. We do not know as far as he is concerned and neither do we know where other psychoanalysts stand. So I do not know where I stand either. Maybe you can help me to find out?

FIVE

The intuition of the negative in *Playing and Reality*

In 1993, I tried to introduce a new concept—"*le travail du negatif*" [the work of the negative]—in a book I published at the time (Green, 1993). In the introductory chapter of that book, I declare that one of the sources that guided me in my elaboration was Winnicott, to whom I was indebted. I mentioned specifically *Playing and Reality* (1971b), the twenty-fifth anniversary of which we are celebrating at this conference. This is the point I am going to illustrate in this lecture, in showing how he inspired me.

If a possible relationship between Winnicott's ideas and mine can be found, this has not been recognized yet. The first time I mentioned the unnoticed importance of the negative in Winnicott's work was during the discussion of a Conference of English-Speaking Members of European Societies in London in October

---

This paper was presented on 6 April 1997 before the International Congress, "The Psyche–Soma: From Paediatrics to Psycho-Analysis", Milan, celebrating the 25th anniversary of the publication of *Playing and Reality*. Reprinted by permission from *The International Journal of Psycho-Analysis*, 78 (1997): 1071–1084.

1976. Masud Khan, the unquestionable expert on Winnicott, replied publicly that I had misquoted Winnicott and that he never said or wrote anything of the sort. Those who knew Khan will not be surprised by such a radical but unfortunately wrong statement. The idea is still so surprising that if you turn to two recent dictionaries on Winnicott's work, written by Alexander Newman (1995) and Jan Abram (1996), there is no trace of the negative. So the question arises: "Is it an invention of André Green?"

Let us go back to *Playing and Reality*. In the first sentence of the Introduction, Winnicott writes: "This book is the development of my paper 'Transitional Objects and Transitional Phenomena' (1951)." So if we read that article carefully, we shall be able to find the thread, whether apparent or invisible, that runs through the whole book. In fact, this paper has a particular history. It is dated 1951, in its initial version.[1] This text would later become the first chapter of *Playing and Reality* (1971b), in a modified form bearing the same title. The 1951 paper appears in 1971 as the first section of the chapter under another title—"Original Hypothesis"[2]—with two new sections, entitled: "II. An Application of the Theory" and "III. Clinical Material: Aspects of Fantasizing", in which the negative is introduced. Section II had already been published in 1960 and 1965, separately. This section starts with a few lines of introduction, followed by a subsection: "Psychopathology manifested in the area of transitional phenomena". The beginning of this subsection substantially modifies the last lines of the 1951–1953 paper, in which Winnicott had initially written about the application of his ideas in psychopathology—that is, "addiction, fetishism and pseudologia fantastica and thieving". In *Playing and Reality* these applications are suppressed, and instead Winnicott focuses on separation and loss. He brings the idea of a limited tolerance to separation in terms of the duration of the separation from the mother object.

---

[1] The paper was read at the British Psycho-Analytical Society on 30 May 1951 (first publication, 1953; second publication, 1975).

[2] In this last version the final lines about psychopathology are omitted. So is the discussion of Wulf's paper on "Fetishism and Object Choice in Early Childhood" (1946). We shall come back to the significance of this self-censorship or change of mind.

He continues with a clinical example, entitled "string".[3] Section II of *Playing and Reality* ends with an "added note 1969", which is included here in this new context, published posthumously in the book.

* * *

Much of what I will have to say is borrowed from the clinical material (Section II), which is entirely new, in this last version of the paper. But there is a long preparatory phase to the new ideas of the book that is already present in the 1951 paper before the explicit idea of the negative develops and is integrated in this seminal paper. The clinical material is supposed to show "how the sense of loss itself can become a way of integrating one's self-experience" (Winnicott, 1971b, p. 20). Here the explicit references to the negative have to do with a pathological structure, but in my view there are other aspects of the notion in the paper which are linked with Winnicott's ideas on normal development and can be found in the beginning of the chapter and in the 1951 version of the paper.

For example, defining the transitional object as a "*not*-me possession" proposes an angle to the concept of object different from its usual positive connotations either as a need-satisfying object, as an object of desire, or as a fantasized object. The object is here defined as a negative of "me", which has many implications with regard to omnipotence. To distinguish between the first object and the first "not-me possession", as Winnicott does, extends our thinking, especially if this is located in an intermediate area between two parts of two bodies, mouth and breast, which will create some third object between them, not only in the actual space that separates them, but in the potential space of their reunion after their separation. This, also, because it implies the idea of something that is not present, is another meaning of the negative. This notion of a "third" object has its application in the analytic situation. I have proposed that we understand the exchanges between patient and analyst or, in other words, between transference

---

[3] This subsection has been published separately. Winnicott gives two references: *Child Psychology and Psychiatry, Vol. 1* (1960) and *The Maturational Processes and the Facilitating Environment* (1965).

and countertransference processes, as creating an "analytic third", a specific outcome of analysis (Green, 1975) This idea has been developed since by Ogden (1994a, 1994b) and Gabbard (1997).

The creation of the transitional object is important: "not so much the object used as the use of the object" (Winnicott, 1971b, p. xii). Winnicott here alludes to the paradox involved in that use—a paradox, as he said, that has to be accepted, tolerated, and respected without forced attempts to solve it. That paradox—no attention has been paid to this—includes a tolerance of the negative, as is mentioned in his section on symbolism. Winnicott writes: "Its not being the breast (or the mother), although real, is as important as the fact that it stands for the breast" (1971b, p. 6). Let us notice, in this same section, an expression of great significance: opposing fantasy and fact, internal and external objects, primary creativity and perception, he states that the term "transitional object" refers to *symbolism in time*. It describes the infant's journey from the purely subjective to objectivity, and it seems to me that the transitional object (piece of blanket, teddy bear, etc.) is what we see of this *journey of progress towards experiencing* (p. 14, italics added).

Instead of being tempted to focus on the opposite terms, which is what any fast reader of Winnicott will be tempted to do, or even the space between them, I shall draw our attention to the idea of the journey. I will come back to it later. The journey expresses the dynamic quality of the experience, implying a move in the space linked with time. I shall dare to suggest that Winnicott develops here an alternative to Freud's theory of the drive that includes a similar change in the space from the source to the object. Let us remember, the transitional space is not just "in between": it is a space where the future subject is *in transit*, a transit in which he takes possession of a created object in the vicinity of a real external one, before he has reached it.

* * *

From this conception of normal development, Winnicott's work focuses progressively on another conception of the negative. Until then the negative was a quality inherent to psychic functioning— for instance, *not-me* possession, the paradox of not being and being the breast as well and at the same time being a substitute for it, not being an internal object or an external one but a "possession", etc. From now on Winnicott is going to describe some pathological issues that need a "complex statement" (1971b, p. 9).[4] The infant can employ a transitional object when the internal object is alive and real and good enough (not too persecutory). But this internal object depends for its qualities on the existence and aliveness and behaviour of the external object. *Failure of the latter in some essential function indirectly leads to deadness or to a persecutory quality of the internal object*" (p. 9).[5] After a persistence of inadequacy of the external object, the internal object fails to have meaning to the infant, and then, and then only, does the transitional object become meaningless too (pp. 9–10).

In the 1951 paper, Winnicott gives the example of two brothers, the elder, X, having failed to form a transitional object. He has an early and persistent attachment to the mother herself. Though he could adopt a rabbit (a toy), the object never had the quality of a transitional object. So it is not only the presence or the absence of an object that looks like a transitional one that is meaningful but the presence or absence of the signs that indicate its quality as such. Winnicott points out that X never married. His younger brother, Y, sucked his thumb, weaned without difficulty, adopted the blanket, used the wool to tickle his nose, invented words to designate his blanket, and is now a father. Both are "normal", but the differences are striking. These remarks pave the way to the added sections of the paper in the *Playing and Reality* version devoted to psychopathology. Winnicott then seems to understand—in contrast to what he wrote in his 1951 paper, where the notion is scarcely mentioned—the prime importance of the absence in the psychopathology of the transitional area. He writes: "If the mother is away over a period of time which is beyond a certain limit measured in minutes, hours, or days, then the memory of the internal representation fades. As this takes effect, the transitional

---

[4] Winnicott is thinking here of the connection between what he says and Melanie Klein.

[5] The 1951 text has been modified here, as Winnicott notes for the reader. The original mentioned the word "badness" before the term "failure". "Badness" disappears in *Playing and Reality*, probably because it is too evocative of Melanie Klein's terminology.

phenomena become gradually meaningless and the infant is unable to experience them. *We may watch the object becoming decathected* (p. 15, italics added). This fading of the internal representations is what I relate to the inner representation of the negative—"a representation of the absence of representation", as I say, which expresses itself in terms of negative hallucination or in the field of affect of void, emptiness, or, to a lesser degree, futility, meaninglessness.

These observations precede the beautiful, moving, and finally tragic example of the string, which I will not comment on again here. The omnipresence of the string in the child's play—a squiggle game played with Winnicott—led him to a conclusion about his little patient that he communicated to the mother. "I explained to the mother that this boy was dealing with a fear of separation, attempting to deny separation by his use of a string, as one would deny separation from a friend by using the telephone" (p. 17). This was an explanation that the mother found silly but that she could, on second thoughts, use. The string was a positive materialization of an absent, negative bond.

In the footnote added in 1969, Winnicott sadly confesses, a decade after the case was first reported, that the child could not be cured of his illness. The denial of his fear of separation was not only linked with his mother's absence while she was hospitalized but also, and even more, with the absence of contact with her when she was physically present.[6] She (the mother) made the very significant comment that she felt the most important separation to have been his loss of her when she was seriously depressed: it was not just her going away, she said, but her lack of contact with him because of her complete preoccupation with other matters (p. 17). In consequence, the child would never accept physical separations from the mother later on.

* * *

We are now ready to come to the more explicit idea of the negative, referring to the last section of the chapter. Until now we have

---

[6] One understands here that the concept of absence has to be understood beyond its manifest meaning.

had to deduce the notion from the text—from now on, as we will see, the notion will be openly expressed.

Winnicott exposes the material from *one* session of an adult patient, a woman. The patient starts reporting a dream in which *the present analyst is seen as an avaricious dominating woman*, which leads her to regret a former analyst seen as a male figure for her. She fantasizes intensely—about catastrophic anxieties related to journeys—on the impossibility of letting other people know what misfortunes happened to her, on being heard crying or screaming, the object being always out of reach. Winnicott states: "Much of the material in this analysis has to do with coming to the negative side of relationships" (p. 21). This included the patient's own experience as a child, and experiences with her children, whom she had to leave for a holiday. On her return she was told that the child had cried for four hours. Winnicott interprets the situation as traumatic, as no explanation can be given to a two-year-old child or to a cat of the absence of the mother. This leads to an experience where the mother is "dead" from the point of view of the baby. After a certain limit of time, the mother is definitely dead, whether absent or present. This means no contact can be re-established when she is back. "This is what dead means", says Winnicott. Winnicott's work is here very close to mine in my description of "The Dead Mother" (1983). It is important to link two extremes, which are very different: "the death of the mother when she is present and her death when she is able to reappear and therefore to come alive again" (Winnicott, 1971b, p. 22). The separation is irreversible, and the tendency to re-experience it is as strong as the manifestation of a drive in repetition compulsion, I would say.

During World War II the patient, then aged eleven, was evacuated (very far from her home). She completely forgot her childhood. But, on the other hand, she was strongly opposed to calling the people who took care of her "uncle" and "auntie", as the other children did in their new families. She managed *"never to call them anything"*, says Winnicott, "and this was the *negative of remembering* her mother and father" (p. 22, italics added).

These many examples of the negative show how close Winnicott was to a notion that he never had a chance to promote to a theoretical status. His readers also. All that refers to a lack: absence of memory, absence in the mind, absence of contact, absence of feeling alive—all these absences can be condensed in the idea of a gap. But that gap, instead of referring to a simple void or to something that is missing, becomes the substratum for what is real. Winnicott says the only real thing is the gap: "that is to say the death, the absence or the amnesia" (p. 22). When the patient experiences an important amnesia during the session, Winnicott writes "that the important communication for me to get was that there could be a blotting out, and that this blank could be the only fact and the only thing that was real. The amnesia is real, whereas what is only forgotten has lost its reality" (p. 22). One can easily make the difference here between what has been blotted out, or, in my own terms, has undergone a negative hallucination, and what is only forgotten, or, in Freud's terms, repressed.

At one point in the session, the patient remembers that there is a rug in the consulting-room that she once put around herself in a period of regression. But now she will not use it any more. "The reason is that the rug that is not there (because she does not go for it) is more real than the rug the analyst might bring, as he certainly had the idea to do" (p. 22). I would add that not using the rug is an absolute necessity. It is a fact to which she will come back at the end of the session, at the point of leaving Winnicott, telling him that the rug could be comfortable, but reality is more important that comfort. She shows also that using the rug would be a sign of forgiveness or that reparation has occurred. If so, the reality of the revenge would fade. But this is mine, not Winnicott's.

In the end, the patient's attitude culminates in the idea that the former analyst (of whom she complained so much) will always be more important to her than the present one (himself). The patient is able to recognize that Winnicott does her more good, but has to confess that she likes the former better. The patient here characterizes the situation in a sentence that recalls Freud: "The negative of him is more real than the positive of you" (p. 23). In her elaboration, the patient would say: "I suppose I want something that never goes away" (p. 23). This is obvious, but what is missing here is that it is the bad object that never goes away. *And the bad thing, whether present or absent, is negative anyway in two ways: as bad and as non-existent.* The judgement of attribution and the judgement of existence coincide. The bad thing has to be there, and if it is not, it is this absence equated with void and emptiness that becomes real, more real than the existing objects that are around. "The real thing is the thing that is not here" (p. 24).

The patient was highly gifted intellectually; from the very beginning, Winnicott tells her that the use of her intellect reflected a fear of mental defect. In fact, the symbols she used could be real for a time, but in the end they faded away. There were reasons to think that she had been anxious because of the appearance of a schizophrenic condition in her environment.

One could see how this concern was linked with uncontrolled aggression and threat of disintegration. Instead, the patient had organized devices to master the destruction. The patient told Winnicott that she used to pull the legs off a paper spider every day her mother was away—a spider that could be used as a daisy to test love. On the other hand, denial of separation could be seen in her relatives. The mother of the patient, wanting her child to feel guilty of always complaining and bothering her, told her that when she was two-and-a-half years old, "we 'heard' you cry all the time we were away" (p. 24)—that is, four miles away. She could not admit that her mother was lying to her—maybe she thought she was omniscient. It could give her the feeling that she was not separated from her if she still heard her.

Symbolization was obviously present but needed to be understood specifically. There was much evidence of its manifestations. But, as Winnicott says, the patient gradually had *"to doubt the reality of the thing that they were symbolising"* (p. 24).

All her life, the patient was haunted by the fear of losing animals, her own children, all her possessions. This was formulated in the sentence: "All I have got is what I have not got" (p. 24). Winnicott comments: "The negative is the only positive" (p. 24). When asked by the patient what he would do about it, Winnicott first remained mute and then said: "I am silent because I don't know what to say" (p. 24), an answer that pleased the patient, probably because the analyst confessed his impotence. It also recognized her ability to protect her mind from his intrusiveness, which led to a triumph of annihilating him.

All this material comes from one session. At the end of it, leaving the analyst and having to go on a railway journey to her holiday house, she expressed the idea that Winnicott could come with her, halfway. After a while the separation would no longer matter. She mocked Winnicott's maternal identification and imagined him on the train, overwhelmed by a lot of babies and children climbing over him, vomiting on him, which was what he deserved. It is evident that she used him to project on him all the bad objects that she had contained during the session and that she could imagine spitting out, after the session, during the journey to her holiday house.

She finally said that when she was evacuated during the war, she went to that other country wanting to see if her parents were there. She seemed to have believed she would find them there. Only after a year or two did she realize that they were not there and "that was reality" (p. 5).

* * *

While I was preparing this, I remembered that I had in my notes the clinical material of a session with a patient that I presented in a seminar on the *"travail du negatif"*, in 1987, long before I wrote my book (1993a). I went back to it. Before reporting the session, I need to give a few words of explanation about my meeting with the patient. During the year I was teaching at University College London, a lady asked to see me. She had attended my inaugural lecture and remembered that she had been advised to see me by one of her friends. The friend told her she had to see me because I was a kind of French Winnicott, a compliment that I was far from deserving. This patient told me she had been in treatment with Winnicott for some years. She had abandoned the treatment with him and, some time later, Winnicott died. She was very distressed not to be able to continue with anyone else after several attempts that failed.

She had had her first analysis when she was young, making many sacrifices and considerable efforts, but the analysis ended very badly in a negative therapeutic reaction. The treatment was stopped by the analyst, who had had enough of her. Before finding Winnicott, she had been to many analysts and therapists of all kinds, whom she abandoned sooner or later. And finally she found

Winnicott. She obviously had an extraordinary impression of their meetings, and she used to tell me, "No one is like Winnicott", which I was very ready to believe.

After our meeting, she seemed to be willing to ask me for some help, though we both knew it was impossible to have a proper analysis with me as we lived in different towns. Even at the time I was teaching in London, I travelled back and forth each week from Paris to London. So, after having interviewed her a few times, I proposed that I would see her for a week or so, three or four times a year. I knew that, especially with this kind of patient, it was very inappropriate, and that she would suffer a lot from our separation. But I had the feeling that the contact that we had during these first interviews was of a sufficient quality (today I would say that I had been seduced) and could maybe be used during our encounters to help her understand what was going on with herself. Anyway it seemed impossible for me to refuse to help her, which she could only experience as a rejection. She accepted what I proposed, and what I had predicted happened. Being in an intense state of suffering in her chronic depressive illness, and having to cope with the fact that I could not see her at the time, I suggested that she should see someone in London in the meanwhile. She tried to meet the colleague I highly recommended, but for all sorts of reasons things could not be worked out. This was both because of her very negative feelings towards him and also because he would not accept a situation that placed him in the position of an intermittent substitute therapist, as she did not mean to stop the relationship with me.

I realized afterwards that I had made a mistake, proposing a solution that neither of them were prepared to accept. It took me some time to realize that my patient was the one Winnicott wrote about in the last section of "Transitional Objects and Transitional Phenomena" (1951). Rereading that section, I felt in total agreement with everything that Winnicott said. I had the great luck of having a living experience of what was described in the paper—a chance that I felt was unique. There were no disagreements with anything I had read, only regrets that Winnicott did not state some facts that seemed to me very important and to which I will come back later. So let me give you the material from one session I had with this patient 10 years ago, at least 15 years after the one reported in Winnicott's book.

The patient would be very concerned to be totally isolated with me. She would start at any noise, and could not bear to hear the bell ring or the telephone. She seemed in a state of terror, but I also felt terrorized by her reactions. She seemed to be confused, looking all around her, as if everything were strange. She would not lie on the couch or sit on the chair in front of me; she sat on the couch and would always start the session by saying: "Where am I? What time is it? What am I doing here?" Then, after a silence, she would begin to speak.

"Let me tell you a dream. *My first analyst comes to visit me. After a while I think he's going to leave, but I realize he won't. So I have to cope with that situation, and then I bend over him to kiss him.*" (This was the analyst whose negative was more real than the positive of Winnicott. I had some idea that at the beginning of the session I might represent him. But I was not so sure he was truly a male figure for her.) She continued, saying that after that dream I had called her to tell her that she could come to see me. (She had phoned earlier to see if this was possible, and I had to check before giving her a positive response.) "One thing that makes me happy is that I gave up all my therapies [drugs] and I feel much better."

A: You do not need any therapy to come to see me.

P: Yes. But what am I doing?

A: Continuing something, maybe.

P: Oh yes, I suppose this must be true. I think that many of my problems have to do with a situation about which something I say is here and with something else which is there, and there is between these two things a space in which something happens like travelling, going there and coming back. "What can I do to go from here to there? Who is here and who is there? And above all, how do I come back?"

You will easily recall how these words remind us of what Winnicott said in terms of facts and events. But here she is speaking of a mental state coinciding with her visiting me. It is also about the link between Winnicott and me. We can think that coming to Paris to see me can also be associated by her to the period where she was evacuated abroad. But even more, I pinpoint the metaphor of the journey as characterizing what goes on in the intermediate area between subjective creativity and objective reality. An important concern is about being able to come back—in other words, not to be lost in some desert, or in the middle of the ocean. The Greeks had a terrifying dread: of losing the way back. In fact, here she seems to be lost in the middle, not reaching anywhere. She told me about the risk of those children dying during the journey (because of the German attacks). After having stayed there for three years, she had changed so much, physically and morally, that when she came back home, her mother had not recognized her—as if her mother had also lost her.

She continued, saying: "I had an interesting experience. I have met two friends who were with me during the evacuation. They loved my mother, and one has even said: 'How I wish she could be my mother!' She always had a photograph of my mother with her. For me she was such an awful, horrible mother, I could not understand. Well, I have been told that my mother did not behave with her own children as she did with the children of others. She must have been so different with them than with me."

I told her that could also have something to do with the "here" and "there": "Maybe it was as if you were not sure that you were the same person in the two places, 'here' and 'there'. Just as it is difficult for you to bring together the two mothers, the mother who is with the others and your own mother."

P: Yes. I have no memory before my leaving. But I have the impression that when I was there in the country I was evacuated to, it was as if my heart was plucked out and put aside and that life had continued. When I came back at 15, my hair was curled, I had lipstick on, and I wore high heels. She did not recognize me.

A: Many things can change between 12 and 15.

P: Oh yes, of course; I had my periods. But that hadn't changed anything for me. I'm going to tell you something which I'm sure you don't know. Elizabeth Taylor has just written a book and appeared on television. She lost two stone, and she has given up everything: drinking, treatment, and the rest. [This reminded me of her giving up the drugs.] Can you imagine, I had a dream. During the war, every week we had an afternoon tea, to which we invited soldiers and danced with them. *And she, Elizabeth Taylor, in the dream, danced with my mother.* Strange, isn't it? It is as if I couldn't leave my parents. When I think of them, I have the feeling they beseech me: "Please allow us to leave, let us go." But it is as if I couldn't.

A: Yes, that's the problem with losing two stone. [What I was alluding to were the two graves of her parents, and communicating to her that it was her parents' body in her own body.]

P: I never understand what you say. [She used to say that either about what she called my Freudian interpretations or about the metaphorical style of them.]

P: In fact when I think of my mother in me it is as if she is petrified. And the more time goes by, the more I am confronted with the necessity of accepting my parents' death, and the more there is something in me which cannot admit they exist no more. It is as if I held them as prisoners in a sort of purgatory or in limbo. [Her parents have been dead a long time.]

A: I think I remember that limbo is the place where dead babies stay. [She and her mother had both lost babies.]

P: Oh, yes. Non-baptised children.

She goes on talking of her first pregnancy, which ended in a miscarriage. The fact that she had been pregnant was taken very badly by her family.

In the session we could witness once again the deep link between her mother and herself, as her mother, too, had had a stillborn baby before the patient's own birth. She says, about her own dead child, that never will she be able to consider him as not existing any more. Again, mourning is impossible; there is a mutual persecution between her and the dead.

INTUITION OF THE NEGATIVE   99

P: I have the feeling that my problem is all a question of space and time. But I feel a little bit better because I don't hang on to my therapists any more, insisting on them making me feel good. I understand that I must not ask them that any more. But going and coming back still raises problems. I cannot travel freely, because I always have to make sure when I travel that I can go to the loo. If I have to make a journey in a bus that has no loo, then I give up. All my thinking tries to connect: "I go there, I take a connection here, I arrive there, I do this, I do that, I can only leave this way." She was looking for a place in the transitional area where she could deposit parts of her body, as if the bond between her and her mother was always there. [Winnicott made the remark that faeces could also be understood as transitional objects.]

* * *

The comparison between the two sessions is remarkable. One will be struck by the significant place of sexuality in the exchange with me and its total absence with Winnicott. This is not only due to the difference in the transference. In fact, one can ask oneself if there was not an important censorship on sexuality in Winnicott's paper. In the 1951 version of the "Transitional Object" paper, there is a substantial discussion of Wulf's paper, "On Fetishism and Object Choice in Early Childhood" (1946), in which Winnicott considers the relationship between fetishism and the transitional object. This useful discussion disappears from the version published in *Playing and Reality*. I happened to know that the patient had been married to a sexually disturbed man, from whom she was now divorced. (Winnicott does not say anything about that; is it only for reasons of confidentiality?) She interrupted her analysis in order to have a love affair. This could not be excluded from the transference relationship. Moreover, during adolescence she had a very intense emotional relationship with her father, who recognized her femininity, causing jealous reactions in her mother. But she resented her father because he did not fully appreciate her intellectual abilities. It does not seem right to me to consider these aspects of the material as a simple defence or even as irrelevant or of no importance. When she came to me, she made all sorts of comments that people in the hotel where she was staying made innuendoes that she came to see a lover in Paris. But in fact in the Elizabeth Taylor dream she represents a homosexual relationship with her mother. I suppose Elizabeth Taylor represented the 15-year-old girl coming back, expecting to seduce the mother. In fact, she was rebuked by her. If there was no dream, I would be tempted to consider this as superficial material. But I do not think it is, as it is clearly shown that the sexual transference to her first analyst is followed by the homosexual fantasy of dancing with her mother.

There is also a journey in the girl's sexual development in what Freud calls the change of object from mother to father. Anyhow, the elements of Winnicott's session are still there. The reference to the journey, to the amnesia, to the telling of having lost her parents, mainly her mother, and above all, the idea of the journey associated to her being two different persons, at the start and in the end, the losing of the sense of continuity, the unacceptance of death, as if the bodies of her parents, and especially of her mother, were petrified in the cage of her own body (dead incorporations)—all this still refers to the work of the negative and the considerable pain of investing positively the relationship with others. This patient would wake up in the morning and spend a long time, moaning "I can't, I can't" for hours before she could get out of bed. The model of the journey seems to be like a dynamic representation of herself, a kind of ultimate attempt to fight the impression of dying in the gap or the void, recalling many things about which she complained at the beginning of our encounters.

During one of our separations, her cat escaped from the house, crossed the street, was hit by a car, and died. She felt an intense pain and wrote to me about what had happened. There were suggestions that the crushed cat lying on the ground could look like an abortion or even faeces. I do not understand very well what that meant for her. In her letters, when she described the corpse of the poor cat, I could not avoid feeling that there was a kind of unconscious satisfaction of which I think she was totally unaware. If I had interpreted this, I believe our relationship would have ended. Obviously the dead cat was a mother–baby animal. The accident had happened while she was away, so it was her fault—as what might have happened to her was her mother's fault. Is it one and the same, after having travelled so far?

In the work I have done with her, I have tried to take up again everything about her relationship with her mother that had been worked through with Winnicott. But I progressively introduced the relationship with the father with all its related gratifications of eroticism and cultural exchange from which her mother was excluded. Her intellectual activity was obviously driven by an identification with the father. We went as far as we could under the circumstances. She even managed to come for nearly a month in order to have intensive treatment, though I warned her that I did not feel that I was omnipotent enough to cure her with that kind of magic therapy. But I am struck with the comparison of what she said to Winnicott at the end of the session he reports, and what she had said to me about travelling on the metro and being confronted with the vomiting of some passengers and going back to London. In fact, as Winnicott told her once, it was as if she had never eaten anything. That infuriated her: she stopped the session and left.

Finally she came for some years less and less frequently, until she stopped seeing me because she did not feel the need to come any more. She always sends me postcards at Christmas, ironically, "as all polite English people do". She was still travelling a lot, but felt better, though not entirely free of symptoms.

* * *

Paradoxically, there is more in Winnicott's clinical material about my ideas on the negative than in my own session. Or, to put it differently, it is more explicitly shown in Winnicott's presentation. There are many reasons for that. Maybe the patient was more disturbed when she had that session with Winnicott than when she had hers with me. Maybe, also, because Winnicott wrote that chapter having in mind his ideas on the negative, which unfortunately he did not have the time to develop. As for myself, I only wrote the book *Le travail du negatif* (1993a) some five years later and did not use the session for this purpose. But in both sessions, Winnicott's and mine, I have tried to link the normal aspects of the negative with the pathological ones. In Winnicott, the normal aspects are shown in the transitional objects—the first "not-me" possession, the paradox of being and not being the breast, etc. In my own case, I tried to reinterpret basic concepts of psychoanalysis to show how the negative is implicit in them.

For instance, the unconscious implies a reference to the negative, not only because it is not conscious but also because in Freud's descriptions, when he thinks of the relationship between two conscious representations in a free-association context, he has to postulate the existence of an unconscious thought or representation between them. Here the negative is associated with the idea of the latent operating behind the scenes, invisible though active. One can even refer to a meaning that would make us think of a photograph, the negative being the element through which the positive can appear. Moreover, apart from this explicit example, some other concepts refer to a similar structure. I think here of identification, seen, in some instances as the opposite of an object relationship. Or, to put it more clearly, that there could be an opposition between all the relationships based on desire, or implying a bodily contact, which I think would deserve to be called positive, and on the other hand the processes operating on distant relationships, with no contact except the one established in the mind, as in identification. In this last instance, the processes could be categorized as belonging to the negative. These are just a few examples of how the negative can be present in very ordinary concepts.

What we have to keep in mind is that in Freud's theory of the drives there is always an implication of something in excess in the psychic apparatus, which has to be reduced or repressed or, I would say, "negativated". This applies to Freud's statement according to which neurosis is the negative of perversion. Winnicott's references are different because he is mainly concerned with separation, a phenomenon that occurs in normal as well as in pathological development. He is mainly oriented towards the object, while I consider the situation from the point of view of the presence of the drives. Anyhow, the reference to absence (common to Lacan and Winnicott) is directly related to the negative as that which is not present, not positively perceived through the senses.

I will propose another model that will account for the normal, "positive" aspects of the negative. When we think of the early mother–child relationship in Winnicottian terms, we realize the importance of holding. When the separation occurs, the baby is left alone. The mother's representation may be suspended and replaced by many substitutes. What is of the greatest importance is the introjected construction of a framing structure [*structure encadrante*], analogous to the mother's arms in the holding. This framing structure can tolerate the absence of representation because it holds the psychic space, like Bion's container. As long as the framing structure "holds" the mind, the negative hallucination can be replaced by hallucinatory wish-fulfilment or fantasy. But when the baby is confronted with the death experience, the frame becomes unable to create substitute representations—it holds only the void. This means the non-existence of the object or of any substitute object. The negative hallucination of the object cannot be overcome, the negative does not lead to an alternative positive substitution. Even the badness of the object and fantasized destructiveness will not do. It is the mind—that is, mental activity giving birth to representations—which is under the threat of being destroyed in the frame. At other times it is the framing structure itself that is damaged: here we have disintegration.

Winnicott's ideas come very close to mine when we consider the pathological issues. We both agree, for instance, that as a consequence of unbearable separation, that which is usually described in terms of aggression, anger, destruction, etc. can manifest itself in a very different way. In his words, what happens is a "fading of the internal representation", and in mine, a destructive negative hallucination of the object. We both think that the mechanism operating here is decathexis. When Winnicott speaks of the negative side of relationships, he means "the gradual failure that has to be experienced by the child when the parents are not available" (1971b, p. 21). This lack of availability of the parents gives rise to two different experiences. One is the feeling of the badness of the object with all the aggression included in crying, screaming, being in a state of agitation and turmoil: here the negative is identified with the bad as the converse of the positive, namely the good. Otherwise this unavailability is related to the non-presence of the object. You will notice that I do not use the word absence, because in the word absence there is the hope of a return to the presence. It is also not a loss because this would mean that the loss could be mourned. The reference to the negative in this second instance is to the non-existence, the void, the emptiness, in other words, the blankness. These two aspects should be differentiated. Winnicott's contribution is to show how this negative, the non-existence, will become, at some point, the only thing that is real. What happens afterwards is that even if the object reappears, the realness of the object is still related to its non-existence. The return of the presence of the object is not enough to heal the disastrous effects of its too long absence. Non-existence has taken possession of the mind, erasing the representations of the object that preceded its absence. This is an irreversible step, at least until treatment.

What is described here is constant in these cases, many of them presenting negative therapeutic reaction. In fact, in these cases neither the analyst nor the patient exists periodically in the session. These defences are mobilized each time the material comes closer to anything that is significant. The patient's mind stops registering the interpretations of the analyst. The interpretations are blotted out, the patient says his mind is blank, no associations are produced. The analytic process is paralysed for some time. The "journey" of Freud's work could be described as starting from neurosis as the negative of perversion to the negative therapeutic reaction. In my mind, some aspects of these patients have not been described by Winnicott. One is struck by the fact that they seem so vulnerable, so fragile, and though they have an extreme rigidity and stubbornness, they are animated with hidden feelings of revenge, which they express in an impossibility to change, or to invest new fields of experience. They seem to be bound to repetition compulsion. All this aspect of the relationship is related to what I have called *primary anality* (Green, 1993b), which is differentiated from ordinary anal eroticism because of the narcissistic aspects of the fixation. The end of my session with the patient shows this concern about the loo. It is one of the many indications of these urethral and anal fixations to which Winnicott does not seem to have paid sufficient attention, probably because they belonged to the drives whose role he may have underestimated, focusing his observation on the objects and the space. In fact, I believe that these aspects with the drives have to be considered together with this object relationship, each one enlightening the other.

Winnicott developed some of the ideas I am presenting here in one of his last papers, which appears retrospectively as an important one, for the understanding of his work and for his readers as well. I am talking here of "The Use of an Object" (1968), in which we can witness the enormous amount of destruction that is implied in the repeated annihilation of the object, where the ordinary visible features of aggression are missing.

Winnicott's idea of the transitional objects and transitional phenomena has taught me something more. Speaking of objects, we should not restrict ourselves to our relationships with existing objects (whether internal or external), but we have to think also of the power of the human mind constantly creating new objects—which I call the *objectalizing function* (Green, 1984, 1995).

We not only create objects from our relation with the outside world, but we supply our internal world with the infinite capacity to create objects. Freud understood this in his description of melancholy, where the ego can offer itself as a sacrifice to replace the lost object—or in identification, when, imagining their dialogue, Freud has the ego saying to the id: "Look, you can love me too—I am so like the object" (Freud, 1923b, p. 30). And, finally, in sublimation we create new and non-existent objects. The objects of sublimation are not only the objects that are involved in the process of sublimation but the activity of sublimation itself. The object of the sublimation of the painter is not only the naked body of the woman, but the painting itself. It is painting that becomes our shared object beyond the representation of what is painted: the nude and its origins in the child's experience.

On the other hand, what has been called, probably improperly, death instinct is based on a *disobjectalizing function*—that is, the process by which an object loses its specific individuality, its uniqueness for us, and becomes any object, or no object at all. A raincoat fetishist does not bother about who wears the raincoat; he is only interested in the dead stuff of the raincoat. The disobjectualizing function implies a (negative) decathexis of objects external, internal, or even transitional. The so-called death instinct becomes an inclination to self-disappearance. It is linked less with aggression than with nothingness. Long ago, Bion made the difference between the no-thing and the nothing.

Let us go back for a while to prehistoric representation. This is not speculation, like the earliest mother–baby relationship of which we know very little, in fact. Here we have evidence. Prehistoric man designed all sorts of drawings in his caves: finger paintings, representations of women with large breasts, wild animals, mammoths, rhinoceros, lions, etc. But on some parts of the ceiling of the caves there were other representations: what prehistorians call *negative hands*.

To represent the hands, prehistoric man used two devices. The simplest was to paint the hand and to make an impression on the wall, leaving a direct trace of it. The second was more indirect and sophisticated.

Here the hand that draws does not draw itself. Instead it places it on the wall of the caves and spreads the colours all around it by spitting the colours on the wall. Then the hand separates from the wall, and a non-drawn hand appears. Such could be the result of the physical separation from the mother's body.

Prehistoric man did not wait for us to know what the negative is about.

REFERENCES

Abram, J. (1996). *The Language of Winnicott: A Dictionary of Winnicott's Use of Words*. London: Karnac Books.
Anzieu, D. (1985). *Le Moi-peau*. Paris: Dunod. [English edition: *The Skin Ego*. New Haven, CT: Yale University Press, 1989.]
Benveniste, E. (1967). *Problèmes de linguistique générale*. Paris: Gallimard. *Problems in General Linguistics*. Coral Gables, FL: University of Miami Press, 1974.
Bion, W. R. (1959). Attacks on linking. In: *Second Thoughts*. London: Heinemann, 1967 [reprinted London: Karnac Books, 1987].
Bollas, C. (1989). *Forces of Destiny*. London: Free Association Books.
Davis, M. (1985). Destruction as an achievement in the work of Winnicott. In: *Winnicott Studies, No. 7*. London: Karnac Books, 1993.
Davis, M., & Wallbridge, D. (1981). *Boundary and Space: An Introduction to the Work of D. W. Winnicott*. Harmondsworth: Penguin, 1983 [reprinted London: Karnac Books, 1999].
Freud, S. (1911b). Formulations on the two principles of mental functioning. *S.E. 12*.
Freud, S. (1915c). Instincts and their vicissitudes. *S.E. 14*.
Freud, S. (1917d [1915]). A metapsychological supplement to the theory of dreams. *S.E. 14*.

Freud, S. (1918b). From the history of an infantile neurosis. *S.E. 17*.
Freud, S. (1920g). *Beyond the Pleasure Principle. S.E. 18.*
Freud, S. (1923b). *The Ego and the Id. S.E. 19.*
Freud, S. (1925h). Negation. *S.E. 19.*
Freud, S. (1937d). Constructions in analysis. *S.E. 23.*
Freud, S. (1940a [1938]). *An Outline of Psychoanalysis. S.E. 23.*
Freud, S. (1940b [1938]). Some elementary lessons in psychoanalysis. *S.E. 23.*
Freud, S. (1940e [1938]). Splitting of the ego in the process of defence. *S.E. 23.*
Gabbard, G. O. (1997). A reconsideration of objectivity in the analyst. *International Journal of Psycho-Analysis, 78*: 15–28.
Green, A. (1972). Note sur les processus tertiaires. *Revue française de psychanalyse, 36.*
Green, A. (1975). The analyst, symbolisation and absence in the analytic setting. *International Journal of Psychoanalysis, 56*: 1–22. Also in: *On Private Madness*. London: Hogarth, 1986 [reprinted London: Karnac Books, 1997].
Green, A. (1983). La mère morte. In: *Narcissisme de vie, narcissisme de mort* (pp. 222–253). Paris: Edition Minuit. [English edition: The dead mother. In: *On Private Madness*. London: Hogarth, 1986.]
Green, A. (1984). Pulsion de mort, narcissisme négatif, fonction désobjectalisante. In: *Le travail du négatif* (pp. 49–59). Paris: Editions de Minuit, 1993.
Green, A. (1986). *On Private Madness*. London: Hogarth [reprinted London: Karnac Books, 1997].
Green, A. (1993a). *Le travail du négatif*. Paris: Editions de Minuit. [English edition: *The Work of the Negative*, tr. Andrew Weller. London & New York: Free Association Books, 1999.]
Green, A. (1993b). L'analité primaire dans la relation anale. In: *La névrose obsessionelle* (pp. 61–86). Paris: Monographies de la *Revue Francaise de Psychanalyse*, ed. B. Brusset & C. Couvreur. Paris: Presses Universitaires de France.
Green, A. (1995). L'objet et la fonction objectalisante. In: *Propédeutique* (pp. 229–266). Paris: Editions Champvallon.
Green, A. (1999). *The Fabric of Affect in the Psychoanalytic Discourse*. London: Routledge.
Heimann, P. (1989). *About Children and Children-no-longer: Collected Papers, 1942–1980*, ed. M. Tonnesmann. London: Tavistock.

Kohon, G. (1999). *The Dead Mother—The Work of André Green*. London: Routledge.

Lacan, J. (1955) *The Seminar of Jacques Lacan, Book III: The Psychoses 1955–1956*, trans. R. Grigg; ed. J.-A. Miller. New York: Norton.

Lalande, A. (Ed.) (1968). *Vocabulaire technique et critique de la philosophie*. Paris: Presses Universitaires de France.

Newman, A. (1995). *Non-compliance in Winnicott's Words*. London: Free Association Books.

Ogden, T. (1994a). The analytic third: working with intersubjective clinical facts. *International Journal of Psycho-Analysis, 75*: 3–19.

Ogden, T. (1994b). *Subjects of Analysis*. New York: Jason Aronson.

Peirce, C. S. (1931). *Collected Papers, Vols. I–VIII*, ed. by C. Hartshore & P. Weiss. Cambridge, MA: Harvard University Press.

Phillips, A. (1988). *Winnicott*. London: Fontana.

Sandler, J. (1976a). Countertransference and role responsiveness. *International Review of Psycho-Analysis, 3*: 43–47.

Sandler, J. (1976b). Dreams, unconscious phantasies, and "identity of perception". *International Review of Psycho-Analysis, 3*: 33–42.

Winnicott, D. W. (1945). Primitive emotional development. In: *Through Paediatrics to Psycho-Analysis*. London: Karnac Books.

Winnicott, D. W. (1951). Transitional objects and transitional phenomena. *International Journal of Psycho-Analysis, 34* (1953): 89. In: *Collected Papers: Through Paediatrics to Psychoanalysis* (pp. 229–242). London: Tavistock, 1958 [reprinted as *Through Paediatrics to Psychoanalysis*. London: Hogarth Press and the Institute of Psychoanalysis, 1975; reprinted London: Karnac Books, 1992]. Also in: *Playing and Reality* (pp. 1–25). London: Tavistock, 1971.

Winnicott, D. W. (1960). String: a technique of communication. *Journal of Child Psychology and Psychiatry, 1*: 229–242. In: *The Maturational Processes and the Facilitating Environment* (pp. 153–157). London: Hogarth Press & The Institute of Psychoanalysis, 1965; New York: International Universities Press, 1965 [reprinted London: Karnac Books, 1990].

Winnicott, D. W. (1962). Ego integration in child development. In: *The Maturational Processes and the Facilitating Environment* (pp. 56–63). London: Hogarth Press & The Institute of Psychoanalysis, 1965; New York: International Universities Press, 1965 [reprinted London: Karnac Books, 1990].

Winnicott, D. W. (1963). Communicating and not communicating leading to a study of certain opposites. In: *The Maturational Processes and the Facilitating Environment* (pp. 179–192). London: Hogarth Press & The Institute of Psychoanalysis, 1965; New York: International Universities Press, 1965 [reprinted London: Karnac Books, 1990].

Winnicott, D. W. (1965). *The Maturational Processes and the Facilitating Environment*. London: Hogarth Press & The Institute of Psychoanalysis; New York: International Universities Press [reprinted London: Karnac Books, 1990].

Winnicott, D. W. (1968). On the use of an object and relating through identifications. *International Journal of Psycho-Analysis, 50* (1969): 711. In: *Psycho-Analytic Explorations* (pp. 218–228), ed. C. Winnicott, R. Shepherd, & M. Davis. London: Karnac Books, 1989; Cambridge, MA: Harvard University Press, 1989.

Winnicott, D. W. (1969). The use of an object in the context of Moses and Monotheism. In: *Psycho-Analytic Explorations* (pp. 240–246), ed. C. Winnicott, R. Shepherd, & M. Davis. London: Karnac Books, 1989; Cambridge, MA: Harvard University Press, 1989.

Winnicott, D. W. (1971a). Mirror-role of mother and family in child development. In: *Playing and Reality*. London: Tavistock.

Winnicott, D. W. (1971b). *Playing and Reality*. London: Tavistock.

Winnicott, D. W. (1975). *Through Paediatrics to Psychoanalysis*. London: Hogarth Press and the Institute of Psychoanalysis [reprinted London: Karnac Books, 1992].

Winnicott, D. W. (1986a). The child in the family group. In: *Home Is Where We Start From*. London: Penguin Books.

Winnicott, D. W. (1986b). *Home Is Where We Start From*. London: Penguin Books.

Winnicott, D. W. (1988). *Human Nature*. London: Free Association Books.

Winnicott, D. W. (1989). *Psycho-Analytic Explorations*, ed. C. Winnicott, R. Shepherd, & M. Davis. London: Karnac Books; Cambridge, MA: Harvard University Press.

Wulf, E. (1946). Fetishism and object choice in early childhood. *Psychoanalytic Quarterly, 15*: 450–471.

INDEX

Abraham, K., 23
Abram, J., xi–xviii, 86
absence, xii, xiv–xv, 15, 30, 35, 67, 80,
    89–93, 102–104
  concept of, 90
  and imaginative elaboration, 80
  of mother, 91
  of breast, 5
actualization, xiii, 4, 37
  experience as, 2
aggression, 73, 77, 78, 93, 103, 105
alienation, radical, 21
alpha function, 44, 51
amnesia, 92, 100
  infantile, 2
anality, primary, 104
analytic relationship, and experience
    of non-ego, 32
annihilation, threat of, 24
anxiety function, 35
Anzieu, D., 74
aphasia, 52
archaic fantasies, 24
Aristotle, 70
attraction function, 35

attribution, judgement of, 57

Bacon, F., 70
Benveniste, E., 58
Bick, E., 41
binding, 29–31, 48, 61
  secondary, 31
biology vs. psychology, 40
Bion, W. R., 5, 34, 51, 57, 66, 72, 80
  "Attacks on Linking", 48
  on container, 103
  and contained, 30
  on no-thing vs. nothing, 105
  theory of thinking of, 1, 44, 67
Bleger, J., 47
Bollas, C., 18
borderline personality disorder, 74
British Psycho-Analytical Society, 70

castration anxiety, 80
cathexis, 14, 29–31, 34, 60
  instinctual, 30
concern, capacity for, 76
condensation, 11, 23, 61
conflict-free sphere, 42

container, 30, 103
countertransference, 88
creation function, 35

Davis, M., 77, 78
death instinct, 7, 29, 73, 77, 105
decathexis, 81, 103, 105
denial vs. the negative, 9, 14
depressive position, 76, 77
Descartes, R., 70
destructiveness, 7, 48, 103
disintegration, 74
disinvestment, 81
disobjectalizing function, 105
displacement, 23, 61
drive(s), 15, 20, 34, 42, 53, 54, 71, 72, 91, 104. *See also* instinct(s)
  monism, 43
  partial, 43
  primary, 81
  theory, 88, 102

economic view of metapsychology, 41
ego, xv, 18–27, 33– 37, 63, 72, 105
  body, 31
  cohesion of, 33
  definition, 19–20
  mechanisms, 42
  -psychology, 42
  -relatedness, 18
  and self, 18
  skin-, 74
  subject, 23
  synthetic function of, 21
  use of term, vs. I, self, subject, 19
elaboration, imaginative, 80–82
Eliot, T. S., 72
envy, 8, 15, 77
existence, judgement of, 57
experience, in analytic work, 1–15
external object. *See* object(s): external

Fairbairn, W. R. D., 23, 78
fantasy, 80–82
Farhi, N., xiv, xv
father, xvi, 10–13, 25, 35–36, 80, 91, 100–101
  id function of, 63
  role of, 79

thirdness, 44–47
Ferenczi, S., 80
fetishism, 86, 99
firstness, 50–51, 59–60, 63–65. *See also* secondness; thirdness
  as being, 63
free-floating attention, 32
Freud, A., 57, 72
Freud, S., *passim*
  Beyond the Pleasure Principle, 29
  on body ego, 31
  "Constructions in Analysis", 2, 47
  on death instinct, 7
  on dream vs. hallucination, 5
  drive theory of, 43, 88, 102
  Ego and the Id, 19, 105
  "Formulations on the Two Principles of Mental Functioning", 32
  "From the History of an Infantile Neurosis" (Wolf Man), 52, 53, 56
  on hallucinatory wish-fulfilment, 30
  inner world of, 24
  on instincts, concept of, 74, 76, 77
  "Instincts and Their Vicissitudes", 78
  on judgement of attribution vs. judgement of existence, 7
  "Metapsychological Supplement to the Theory of Dreams, A", 5
  metapsychologies of, 41
  "Negation", 6, 7, 13, 51
  on negation and thinking, 7
  object relations theory of, 29
  on object representations, 22
  on the psychic, 39, 40
  on psychoanalysis as science, 41
  on uncovering of unconscious, 13
  Outline of Psychoanalysis, An, 29, 69
  on psychoanalytic experience, 2
  on role of identification, 22
  on role of the negative, 6
  on setting as closed system, 32
  "Some Elementary Lessons in Psychoanalysis", 39, 40
  "Splitting of the Ego in the Process of Defence", 21

INDEX

theory of psychic apparatus of, 50
theory of representation of, 50
on thing-presentations vs. word-presentations, 6

Gabbard, G. O., 88
Gaddini, R., 40
Green, A., xi–xviii, 35, 85, 86, 88, 104, 105
On Private Madness, xi, xvii

hallucination, 81
  vs. dream, 5
  negative, 5, 30, 90, 92, 103
  positive, 5
hallucinatory wish-fulfilment, 5, 30, 54, 103
Hartmann, H., 41, 42, 57
Hegel, G. W. F., 21
Heimann, P., 71
historical perspective, definition, xiii, 2–4
holding, 30, 102, 103
  handling and object presenting, 30
human nature, concept of, 70

I:
  vs. not-I, 7
  use of term, vs. ego, self, subject, 19
id, 19, 42, 63, 70, 74, 105
idealization, 24
ideational representative, 53, 54, 56
identification, 22, 23, 26, 34, 102, 105
  maternal, 94
  paternal, 101
  projective, 24, 59
identity:
  disorders, 19, 20
  sense of, 19
illusion, 19, 81–83
  function, 35
incarnation, concept of, 73
incorporation, 33
  dead, 100
induction function, 35
infant:
  observation, 41, 71
  progression of, from fusion to independence, 45

infantile amnesia, 2
instinct(s), 26, 28–29, 31, 33–36, 42, 53, 54, 78–82. *See also* drive(s)
  aim-inhibited, 35, 36
  aim-uninhibited, 35, 36
  bud of, 81
  concept of, 74
  destructive, 48
  experience, 79–80
  theory, 73, 76–79
  integration, 74
intellect, 73–76
internal object. *See* object(s): internal
internalization, xv, 30, 33, 58
interpretation, 4, 58, 60, 65, 66, 67, 104
introjection, 15, 33
Isaacs, S., 69

James, H., 70
judgement of attribution, of existence, 57

Keats, J., 67
Khan, M., 86
Klein, M., 23, 41, 57, 72, 76–78, 89
  inner world of, 24
Kohon, G., xvii
Kohut, H., 43

Lacan, J., 21–23, 49–51, 59, 67, 102
  concept of the symbolic, 60
  on function of father, 36
  on mirror stage, 26
  on paternal metaphor, 45
  on role of identification, 22
  on signifier, 49, 50
  and subject, 20, 21
  on splitting, 21
  on subject, 22
  unconscious, 23
Lalande, A., 70
life:
  force, 77
  instinct(s), 29, 48, 77, 81
  links, 33
logic of relatives, 50, 64, 66
loss, xiv, 5, 86, 90, 103
  and integration, 87
love instinct(s), 29, 48, 77, 81

Mahler, M., 41
Marty, P., 74
metapsychology, 41–43
  dynamic view of, 41
  genetic view of, 41
  vs. metaphysics, 43
Mill, J. S., 71
mind, 73–76
mirror stage, 26
Mitchell, J., xvii
mother, *passim*
  –infant relationship, 25–26, 30, 35, 43–44, 46, 80, 102, 105
  absence of, 89, 91
  and child, separation between, 46
  dead, through absence, xvii, 91
  role of, 44
  superego function of, 63

narcissism, primary, 77, 78, 82
negative, the, 3–5, 10, 85–106
  aspects of, xiii
    destructive, 7, 14
    as facilitating the unknown, 14, 15
  concept of, xiv, xiv, xv
  Freud on, 6
  handling of, in transference, 12–13
  photographic, 6
  tolerance of, 88
  work of, xiii, 5, 14, 85, 100
negative capability, 67
negative hallucination, 5, 30, 90, 92, 103
negative therapeutic reaction, 94, 104
neutrality, 32
Newman, A., xi, xii, 86
no-breast, 5
non-ego, 32–33
  unconscious, 33
no-thing, 5, 105
not-I, 7
not-me, 32–33, 74
  possession, 87, 88, 101

object(s), 18–37
  of desire, 21
  external, 18, 24, 25, 55, 88, 89
  function of, 34
  internal, 18, 24, 25, 33, 37, 55, 57, 88, 89
  maternal, 24, 44
  objective, 24
  part, xvi, 24, 36, 77
    significant, xvi
  paternal, 24
  primitive, 37
  relations, 14–15, 18, 20, 23, 28–29, 35, 66, 82, 102, 104
  theory, 18, 29, 73, 76–79
  representation, 22, 56
  unconscious, 59
  and self, 18
  and subject, 17–37
  transitional. See transitional object
  unifying concept of, 24
  whole, 24, 77
objectal vs. *objectif*, 18, 24
objectalizing function, 36, 37, 105
objective perception vs. primary creativity, 51
oedipal structure, 25
Oedipus complex, 43, 63, 73, 76–80
Ogden, T., 88
omnipotence, 47, 82, 87
oral phase, 81

paranoid–schizoid position, 77
Paris Psychosomatics School, 74
Parsons, M., xvii, xviii
part object. See object(s): part
paternal metaphor, 45
Peirce, C. S., xv, 50–52, 57–66
  semiotic theory of, 50
perception, 6, 55–57, 61, 67
  objective, 51
  and primary creativity, 88
  vs. representation, 80
persecution, 24
perversion, neurosis as negative of, 102, 104
phenomena:
  transference, 31
  transitional, 80–82, 90, 105
  unconscious, 40
phenomenology vs. psychoanalysis, 17
Phillips, A., 72

philosophy, 82–83
pleasure principle, 29, 32, 57, 61
potential space, 5, 32, 67, 87
primal scene, xvii, 52
primary anality, 104
primary creativity, 88
  vs. objective perception, 51
primary fantasies, 43
primary processes, 22, 24, 29, 43, 48,
  49, 51, 81. *See also* secondary
  processes; tertiary processes
primary repression, 43
projection, 27, 30–32, 56, 59
psyche, xiii, 2, 27, 29, 40, 42–44, 61, 63,
  72–76
  concept of, 39, 60, 80
  distinctions between, 73
  dwelling of in body, 74
  embodied in body, 72
  and soma, 74
psychic apparatus, 43
psychology vs. biology, 40
psychosomatosis, 74

reality, 82–83
  external, 72–73, 77, 83
  internal, 73
  -testing, 57
rebinding, 48
reflection, function of, 35
regression, 73–74, 81, 92
reparation, concept of, 77, 92
repetition compulsion, 91, 104
representamen, 57–63, 65
representance, 21, 22, 61
representation, *passim*
  body-, 25
  concept of, 6, 50, 55, 57, 61
  internal:
    conscious, 55, 102
    unconscious, 55
  object, 22
  self, 22
representative, ideational, 53, 56
repression, 6, 35, 46, 55
  of forbidden wishes or drives, 42
  and negation, 6
  primary and secondary, 43
reverie, maternal, 44

Sandler, J., xiii
satisfaction function, 35
Saussure, F. de, 49–50, 60
secondary fantasies, 43
secondary processes, 7, 17, 22, 31, 43,
  48–51, 59, 62, 81. *See also*
  primary processes; tertiary
  processes
secondary repression, 43
secondness, 50, 51, 59, 60, 63–65. *See
  also* firstness; thirdness
self [*le soi*], 18–22
  and ego, 18
  independent of drives, 43
  integration of, 72
  and object, 18
  use of term:
    vs. I, ego, 18, 19
    vs. subject, 18
  representation, 22
  separation, 48, 80–81, 86–87, 90–91,
    94, 102–103
  denial of, 93
  fear of, 90
  from mother, 30, 45, 46, 86, 102, 106
  and reunification, 32, 48
setting, analytic, 1, 3, 32, 44, 47, 66
sexuality, 30, 55, 73, 77, 99
  childhood, 79
  in mother–infant relationship, 36,
    46
Shakespeare, W., 75
sign, 50, 52, 58–62, 66
  definition, 59
  and signifier, 49
  thought as manipulation of, 66
signified, 49–50
signifier, 20–21, 49–50, 59, 72
  of the unconscious, 49
soma, 74, 80
soul, 73–76
Spitz, R. A., 41
string, 90
structural view of metapsychology,
  41
subject, 18–28, 33, 35
  concept of, 18
  definition, 20
  and object(s), 17

subject (*continued*):
  relations, 18
  unconscious, concept of, 20–22
  use of term, 18
  vs. ego, I, self, 19
sublimation, 34, 37, 105
substitution function, 35
superego, 19, 63, 70
symbiosis, 47
symbolism in time, transitional object as, 88
symbolization, xvi, xvii, 47–48, 81, 93

tertiary processes, xvii, 22, 48–50, 59, 81. *See also* primary processes; secondary processes
thinking, 44, 52, 62, 67
  in analytic work, 1–15
  art of, xvi
  roots of, 6
  and soma, 80
  and thing-presentations vs. word-presentations, 6
  thirdness, 63
  vs. thoughts, 66
thirdness, xv, xvi, 20, 39–68, 87. *See also* firstness; secondness
  as thinking, 63
topographic view of metapsychology, 41
transference, 21, 28, 33, 61, 67, 87, 99
  negative in, 12
  phenomena, 31
transitional area, 48, 89, 99
transitional object, 37, 41, 81–82, 87–89, 99, 101, 105
  and fantasy, 81
transitional phenomena, xiv, xvii, 80–81, 89, 105
transitional space, 57, 81, 88

trauma, 42

unbinding, 29, 48
unconscious, the, 17
  denial of, 19
unintegration, 74
unpleasure principle, 32, 57, 61
unthought known, xiii

Wallbridge, D., 78
Winnicott, C., 69
Winnicott, D. W., *passim*
  on baby, 43
  "Child in the Family Group, The", 77
  "Ego Integration in Child Development", 74
  on holding, 30
  Human Nature, xvi, 69–83
  "Mirror-Role of Mother and Family in Child Development", 26
  object relations theory of, 78
  Playing and Reality, xiv, xv, 85–106
  on potential space, 32, 67
  "Primitive Emotional Development", 72
  "String", 87, 90
  on symbolization, 47
  on transitional objects, 41
  "Transitional Objects and Transitional Phenomena", xiv, 48, 86–89, 95, 99
  "Use of an Object in the Context of Moses and Monotheism", xvi
  "Use of an Object and Relating through Identifications, On the", 77, 104, 105
Wolf Man, 52, 56
Wulf, E., 86, 99